Jane L. Stanford

Jane Stanford

HER LIFE AND LETTERS

BY
GUNTHER W. NAGEL

STANFORD ALUMNI ASSOCIATION
STANFORD, CALIFORNIA

To Jane L. Stanford's "boys and girls"

Gunther W. Nagel

Foreword

―――――◆―――――

STANFORD UNIVERSITY, its alumni and friends are greatly indebted to Dr. Gunther W. Nagel for this historical account of Jane Stanford's devotion to the institution of which she was co-founder. Dr. Nagel's work bespeaks his own devotion to Stanford, a long-standing and continuing interest in its history, development, and welfare, and, as a result, a wealth of knowledge about his alma mater. Thanks are due also to the Stanford Alumni Association for arranging publication.

It is well for us of later generations to be reminded of Stanford's beginnings. They constituted an adventure in educational pioneering. As the adventure unfolded, it encountered risk, adversity, and sorrow. After Senator Stanford's death, the burden of keeping the fledgling institution on its chartered course fell on the shoulders of Jane Stanford. She accepted that burden and bore it with stouthearted courage and a sustaining, indomitable faith which are revealed—often poignantly—in her letters.

As an institution gains in strength and distinction, as Stanford has done, there may be a too-ready tendency to take for granted the eminence which the University has attained. Such a tendency would be regrettable, because it would invite forgetfulness of the vision and generosity of the founders and the dedication of the first and early faculty members who shared the adventure and who stood by Jane Stanford through her years of trial and loneliness.

In these more populous days of universal suffrage, multiple-choice election ballots, expansive government, and international uncertainties, one may wonder what one individual can do to make his or her vote or work count for good. Granted that the twentieth century has brought manifold and far-reaching change. Even so, this tribute to Jane Stanford stands as a reminder that noble work may yet be wrought by one person. May the reminder not be forgotten, and may Jane Stanford be gratefully remembered.

J.E. Wallace Sterling
Chancellor, Stanford University

vii

Jane Lathrop Stanford, 1881. Léon Bonnat. Stanford University Museum of Art. Gift of Jane Lathrop Stanford.

Introduction

JANE LATHROP STANFORD was an equal collaborator with her husband in planning and founding Stanford University. When Leland Stanford died on the 21st of June, 1893, within two years after the University opened, she alone insured its continued existence against tremendous odds. The worst financial crisis the country had yet experienced and a government suit placed the Stanford estate in a precarious position. Jane's business advisors told her that the University would have to be closed, but, given strength by her faith, she determined to keep its doors open and she overcame the difficulties besetting her path.

As bygone days recede into the ever-deepening shadow of the past, a certain amount of myth becomes intertwined with reality. Fortunately, Jane Stanford has left an extensive record of her thoughts and actions. Her letters during that fateful period disclose with vivid force her aims, her hopes, her trials, her triumph. She has been quoted often to describe some specific event in the history of the University, but her letters and papers heretofore have not been correlated and so made known that she herself is allowed to tell her story.

Letters often reveal a person's character and accomplishments in a truer light than any amount of information gathered by others long after the events of the day are over. This is especially true if they were composed before the dictaphone, the typist, and the telephone intervened to make the handwritten personal letter a lovely relic of the past.

Most of Jane Stanford's letters in the University Archives' collection of Stanford Family Papers are originals, some are handwritten draft copies, and a few are typed. The art of writing in the nineteenth century was undoubtedly affected by the means at hand. At one stop during her travels, Jane attributed her poor penmanship to inferior ink and the lack of a blotter. Nevertheless, with a few exceptions, her handwriting is clear, making the transcription of her letters a painstaking but pleasant task. Especially in personal missives, she was inclined to be careless in spelling and at times took full advantage of the letter-writer's disdain for punctuation. To make for smoother reading, these distractions have been corrected, but great care has been taken not to alter the flow and meaning of her words.

Sincerity and conviction are evident throughout. On occasion she would seek refuge in her "timidity" and "womanly reserve," but her accomplishments as organizer, manager, and builder in what at the time was predominantly a man's world gave proof that she was anything but timid when her cause, the University, was at stake. Jane Stanford's goal to establish the University on a high moral tone and on foundations that would last through the ages was ever kept in mind and no distraction was allowed to divert her from this course.

Jane's religious faith, the product of a Puritan background and up-bringing, in adult life became a dominant characteristic verging on eccentricity and, as her letters reveal, gave her the strength to complete the task she devoutly believed her Heavenly Father had designated her to fulfill. As sympathetic a recorder as Edith Mirrielees, for many years professor of English at the University, described Mrs. Stanford as "embarrassingly ready to summon God into mundane discussions." On the other hand, David Starr Jordan, first president of Stanford, and John Casper Branner, vice-president, were unstinting in their praise of this and every aspect of Mrs. Stanford's being. Readers will be able to judge for themselves from her own words and deeds.

A gentle side of her character is revealed in her friendship with the students, both men and women, and in letters to her good friend May, the wife of Timothy Hopkins. In them she shows interest and pleasure in social interchange and a knack for describing the sights and events of travel abroad, as well as compassion for others when they, too, were troubled.

Jane Stanford's letters tell of the early days of the University while the events were unfolding—at the same time revealing the character of a remarkable woman—and thus have an impact and reality no historian can match.

G.W.N.

Stanford
September 1, 1975

Contents

1

The Mother of a University

———◆———

ONE PLEASANT AFTERNOON in the spring of 1903 Mrs. Leland Stanford stood on the veranda of her home on the edge of the Stanford University campus. She was surrounded by a jolly throng of women students who spilled down the steps and out beneath the nearby oaks. Led by the glee and mandolin clubs, they were serenading her with lilting college songs.

It was a happy occasion. Stanford had just won a spirited contest on the playing field. This pleased everyone, but of greater import to Mrs. Stanford was that ten difficult years had passed since her husband's death. Suddenly alone, and contrary to all expectations, the widow had been beset with overwhelming financial problems. But, despite the dictum of her advisors that the University must be closed, she had almost singlehandedly kept its doors open.

After the worst of the storm that followed Senator Stanford's death had blown over, Mrs. Stanford had enjoyed her role as surviving founder. But now, approaching her seventy-sixth year and believing she had done what she could to place the University on sound physical and spiritual foundations, she thought it best for all concerned to relinquish full control into the hands of the Board of Trustees she and her husband had appointed. This would be accomplished a few weeks hence. For the present the songs, the laughter, the chatter of the young women about her were particularly gratifying because it was she who had convinced her husband to provide for the admission of women at the University, at a time when most private institutions of higher learning were restricted to one sex.

The occasion for Jane's meeting with the women students was that the day had been set apart for them on the campus and named in their honor. Even the operation of the daily student paper was taken over by an all-female staff. Appropriate events had been planned, including this friendly visit with the surviving founder. As the shadows lengthened, youthful voices burst forth with the University hymn, "Hail! Stanford, Hail!" When the last strains had faded away in the twilight, a hush fell. Gently breaking the stillness, Jane Stanford thanked the young women and told them that they exerted an influence far beyond their conception, and she hoped it would always be for good. She assured them she wished each one to enjoy to the fullest her equal privileges, but to do so "with gentle womanly dignity, respecting herself and making all with whom she comes in contact respect her."

The young ladies Mrs. Stanford addressed so warmly in the unfolding twentieth century had broader opportunities than had their predecessors a hundred years before, though Congress had not yet granted them the right to vote. Much had happened to advance the cause of women's rights in Mrs. Stanford's lifetime and she had helped the cause by deed and example. She got to know most of the leaders of the growing suffragist movement, and that her relationship to them was more than just that of a valued supporter is evidenced by letters from the president of the National Woman Suffrage Association, Susan B. Anthony. (The railroad passes referred to were a frequent form of largess, as manifested by numerous thank-you notes in the Stanford files.)

Rochester, N.Y., February 22, 1895

My dear Mrs. Stanford:

At 6:30, while my sister and I were at the tea-table, a boy brought your telegram saying you had sent the passes to dear Mrs. Cooper, and I wired back my thousand thanks. But I want to write them also, and when I get to San Francisco I shall want to speak them too. . . .

2

It is splendid of you to thus renew your kindness of last spring and your devoted husband's to Gloria, Mrs. Stanton, and me of twenty-five years ago! . . . I do hope the educational work we shall do will result in a majority of voters casting their ballots for the Amendment.

Almost the first thing on my arrival, I want an hour of your most valuable time to tell you how we can secure the end we all so much desire. . . . I want to tell you upon what hangs all our hopes—our very fate—but I cannot scribble it, nor could you take the time to read it.

So, my dear friend and helper, good-bye until we meet.

Gratefully and affectionately,
Susan B. Anthony

In the fall Miss Anthony again wrote to Mrs. Stanford hoping that the time had come to give her name as a vice-president of the women's suffrage amendment campaign committee and also that she would be a patron of the National Council of Women. Miss Anthony added, "I wish you, as the pioneer woman to own and manage a great university, would help celebrate Elizabeth Cady Stanton's eightieth birthday." Mrs. Stanton was organizer of the first women's rights convention. The available records do not disclose Mrs. Stanford's response. Another leader in the movement, Rev. Annie H. Shaw, was invited by Mrs. Stanford to speak in the Stanford Chapel.

The California campaign for the state women's suffrage amendment in 1896 was well organized, with nationally-known speakers and wide newspaper support. Mrs. Stanford was among the many prominent persons who contributed to the cause. However, a last minute drive by its opponents, led by powerful and alarmed liquor interests, succeeded in defeating the amendment by a narrow margin.

During the meeting of the National Woman Suffrage Association in San Francisco in 1901 Mrs. Stanford, in a newspaper interview, made clear her own views on women's rights in education and suffrage and gave her reasons for limiting the number of women students at Stanford to 500. Ever since she had implemented that decision about two years previously, she had been flooded with correspondence, most of it friendly, asking her reasons. Probably only a few of her intimate friends knew that it was she who suggested to Senator Stanford that women students be allowed in the University. That was before their plans had been made public. He had thought about the subject himself and they agreed that women should be admitted in full equality. Nevertheless, Mr. Stanford believed the institution should be primarily for men. Neither had foreseen that women might eventually outnumber the men, and so it was solely for faithfully carrying out her late husband's purposes that she made her decision.

"[The University] must not change its character as primarily an institution for young men," Mrs. Stanford declared. "Notwithstanding," she continued, "I favor the education of women, believe in coeducation and, in fact, believe fully in the right of women to have the franchise. Nobody appreciates more than I do the advantages of an education to those of my sex. Nor does anybody realize more than I do the effect on society of an educated and enlightened womanhood. A woman can be educated and even vote, if you please, and still be a womanly woman."

Because of President David Starr Jordan's close association with Jane Stanford during the turbulent years that followed immediately after Senator Stanford's death, when the very existence of the University hung in the balance, he was better able to speak of her qualities than was any other person:

"She possessed great decision of character, a preeminently religious spirit, a high degree of business ability, and a straightforward democratic manner combined with large experience in the world. . . . Her salient personal trait, that of absolute loyalty to every plan of her husband, was of paramount value to us through twelve years in which the University and its future rested absolutely in her hands. Had she yielded or flinched in any one of a dozen crises or embarrassments, the endowment would have been wrecked."

Jane Stanford was stately, of more than average height, and of commanding presence. Extremely neat herself, she disliked carelessness in others and in her surroundings. Her predominantly serious nature is evident in her portraits. Even had an artist or photographer had the temerity to ask her to smile, it is doubtful that she would have complied. The controlling forces of her life and works were implacably serious, yet she had a lighter side. The students recognized her inner warmth and friendliness and she enjoyed their youthful exuberance. *Stanford Stories,* by two alumni, Charles K. Field and Will H. Irwin, was popular reading. Hearing Field referred to as a playboy, Mrs. Stanford said, "I hope he was a playboy while young, but this book holds promise of something fine to come from these two dear boys later on." Both became successful authors. Many students were her friends. She always spoke of them as "my boys and girls."

Unswerving in adherence to her own principles, she was tolerant of

4

others. It was not then considered proper for women to smoke. Once while abroad she met a party of Stanford women several of whom, in a spirit of daring more readily exhibited away from home, were self-consciously puffing cigarettes. Asked if she minded, Mrs. Stanford replied, "No, I don't think it wrong to smoke a cigarette after dinner; I might enjoy toying with one myself but that I am the Mother of a University."

She was not above making a pun on occasion. Andrew A. Browne, assistant professor of mechanic arts and superintendent of shops, had been requested to design grilles for her wine cellar. Glancing up while engaged in measuring the apertures, he was surprised to find Mrs. Stanford standing by observantly. "We meet on a low level, Mr. Browne," she said, to which he replied with Irish aplomb, "That we meet at all is a pleasure." These opening quips led to a lengthy discussion about the University and Professor Browne invited her to visit his shops. To his astonishment she and her brother, Charles Lathrop, came the next day. Professor Browne apologized for his work clothes, but Mrs. Stanford interjected, "If my boy were still alive, this is where he would be."

2

"We will go to California!"

———◆———

$\mathcal{M}$RS. LELAND STANFORD was born Jane Eliza Lathrop in Albany, New York, on August 25, 1828. She was one of six children and her father's favorite. Though she professed not to put much stock in lineage, Jane was nevertheless blessed with a succession of sturdy, self-reliant ancestors culminating in her parents, Dyer Lathrop and Jane Ann Shields. She did single out one forebear for special mention, her great-grandfather, Reverend John Lathrop, minister of Old South Church in Boston, who preached the sermon inciting his hearers to throw the tea overboard in Boston Harbor. Mrs. Stanford became a charter member of the first Western chapter of the Daughters of the American Revolution.

Dyer Lathrop, a successful merchant and socially aware citizen of Albany, was one of the founders of the Albany Orphan Asylum. As soon as Jane was old enough, she accompanied him on his frequent visits to the institution, a walk of some distance. Those trips may well have stirred in the heart of the child some deep feeling which in later years would bring both comfort and hope to many a homeless waif.

Though born to a certain affluence, Jane Lathrop was not pampered. Only the kitchen and dining room of the family home in Albany were heated. The children had after-supper chores, then on winter nights would scamper upstairs to tumble into bed between ice-cold sheets to await the comforting warmth that followed. If some duty had been neglected, their father waited until they were snugly settled before routing them out to complete the task. The lesson was soon learned.

Jane was not robust, but she benefited by farm life with relatives during summer months, where she shared in the outdoor work and learned the feminine domestic arts essential to a family's well-being. She suffered from migraine and for years had weak eyes. These afflictions did not prevent her from acquiring the basic schooling of that day, completed at the Albany Female Academy.

It was during Jane's childhood that the first stirrings of the women's rights movement began in America. An education commensurate with that of men was one of its original goals, and by the time Jane Lathrop began her formal education a wide field was open to her. Jane's name is written in copybook penmanship on the cover of a *Circular and Catalogue* of the Albany Female Academy of 1845, now in the Stanford University Archives. The circular details the system of instruction and the prescribed courses. Orthography, reading, grammar, and arithmetic were emphasized throughout. Particular attention was paid to composition, "this very important branch of female education." The brochure further states that sacred music has been taught in the institution for the last ten years and "its influence upon the pupils has been most happy, considered in reference to its physical, social, or moral tendencies."

Prestigious listings of trustees, professors, courses, method, and objective indicate that schooling in the Academy was a serious and disciplined experience. That Jane Lathrop did not waste her opportunities was evidenced in later years by her extraordinary accomplishments as the surviving co-founder of Stanford University. Her extensive personal and official correspondence and the intricate details involving her University management were given largely in her own hand. These missives show the sharpness of her intellect and the worth of her youthful instruction.

A sincere religious feeling and belief in old-fashioned virtues came naturally with Jane's upbringing. Self-assurance and independence of will were her own possessions. She was not easily intimidated. She liked to dance and one Sunday was publicly reprimanded for this by her preacher. The following week Jane attended a different church.

In due course she was courted by the enterprising neighbor lad who had hauled wood for the Mohawk and Hudson River Railroad. On September 30, 1850, Jane Eliza Lathrop and Leland Stanford were married by the Reverend Luther Beecher in North Pearl Baptist Church, Albany. In the manner of the period, though the members of both families were substantial citizens, only a simple announcement appeared in the *Albany Argus*. The few romantic details that have been handed down are conjecture; the principals kept their innermost feelings sealed.

Leland Stanford's background was quite similar to Jane's. One of six sons, he spent his youth on a farm whose homestead also served as a tavern on the busy Albany–Schenectady Turnpike. The family was a contented and busy one. Both parents believed in rectitude and Yankee industry as the source of the greatest happiness in life. His father's farming and innkeeping were supplemented by bridge building and other construction work, so that Leland gained an insight into skills that stood him in good stead.

The young Stanford completed an ample education for the period at the Cazenovia Seminary, a Methodist coeducational institution not far from Syracuse, New York, following which he became apprenticed to a well-known law firm in Albany and in 1848 was admitted to the bar. The lure of the West induced him to decline an offer to join the firm and instead to open a law office of his own in Port Washington on Lake Michigan in the newly admitted state of Wisconsin. There Leland brought his bride, and Jane, aged twenty-two, set up her own household.

Jane adapted herself willingly to the unaccustomed stern life in a frontier town; but, though things began auspiciously, the Port Washington stay proved only an interlude. Leland was active in community affairs, joined a debating club, was nominated by the Whigs for district attorney, and, though defeated, made a good showing in the overwhelmingly Democratic community. An attempt to start a local paper collapsed because of insufficient funds but his appetite for newsprint had been whetted and he retained henceforth a great respect for the power of the press.

The town did not develop as expected and Jane found little social life in the largely Scandinavian community. Two of Leland's brothers had gone to California to found a mercantile business and their favorable reports made him think seriously of joining them. A disastrous fire in his office settled the matter. Having futilely tried to quench it, Leland came home haggard and disheveled and exclaimed to his anxious wife, "I have lost everything of value I possessed!" Overcome with fatigue and discouragement, he burst out, "What shall we do?" Without a moment's hesitation or weakness, on the inspiration of the moment Jane answered, "We will go to California!"

In complete agreement the young couple returned to Albany to make arrangements for their new adventure. At the very last moment, after the final preparations for the long journey to California had been made, Dyer Lathrop raised strong objections to having his daughter go. He pointed out that there were wild tales about hardship and danger in California, it was a man's world, and Leland should first make his own way. Jane protested vehemently but when her husband, too, accepted her father's arguments, there was nothing for her to do but yield. And so for the following three years Jane again lived in her parental home while her husband, 3,000 miles away, tended store in a rough mining camp, his cot a wooden counter, his boots his pillow.

Jane's drab existence was made additionally depressing by ill-concealed gossip that her husband had forsaken her. The only ray of sunshine came with the regular monthly mail, which always carried an exchange of letters with Leland. Unable to hide the pang these brought her, she read them solely in the solitude of her own room. The letters were treasured for years, but shortly after her husband's death she destroyed them and so hid their secrets forever from prying eyes. Meanwhile, in far more stimulating surroundings, Leland Stanford labored and prospered.

Hearing of the death of his father-in-law in the spring of 1855, Leland hurried East and returned to California with Mrs. Stanford by his side. His three years of sleeping on the counter and Jane's loneliness were over. From that time onward Jane Stanford's story became indissolubly linked with that of her husband. A modest dwelling was obtained and Leland wrote his parents: "We live well. Have plenty of good coffee, bread, meat and potatoes and such other things as we want, but we are both fond of the substantial." They began simply enough, Jane making the curtains and he knocking together a few chairs and a table out of packing boxes.

Leland took over the Stanford brothers' store in Sacramento and built a spacious new one at the corner of L and Front Streets. The next few years were busy, prosperous, and happy ones, until in 1860 Leland announced that he was quitting his business and had decided to settle in the East. The news could scarcely have pleased Jane, but together they went once more to Albany. However, the city had lost its earlier charm and her last memories of it were sad. Her happiest days had been spent in California and it was there she wished to live. Possibly the return of the successful voyager to the haunts of his boyhood had already begun to pall for her husband; at any rate Jane had little difficulty persuading him to accede to her wish. Stanford had been one of the founders of the Republican Party in California, so before returning they visited Washington to attend President Lincoln's inaugural ball.

3

A Stanford Heir Is Born

ON JANUARY 10, 1862, Leland Stanford, not yet thirty-eight years of age, was inaugurated governor of California. The elements chose that day to send the American and Sacramento rivers on one of their frequent rampages. Sections of the capital city, Sacramento, were under five to ten feet of water, but this did not spoil the political or social success of the occasion. The ceremonial ball was a gala affair. Accompanying Governor and Mrs. Stanford were his mother, and also her mother, sister, and brother, Henry Lathrop.

Despite a successful administration during which he was credited with keeping California in the Union, Governor Stanford did not seek a second term. Just after being nominated for the governorship in 1861, he had been named president of the newly incorporated Central Pacific Railroad Company of California, the western section of a contemplated transcontinental line. He now wished to devote all his time to this venture. His partners were Charles Crocker, Mark Hopkins, and Collis P. Huntington. In spite of incredible obstructions placed in its pathway by both man and nature, the Central Pacific pushed its rails over the Sierra. The iron link between East and West was completed in Promontory, Utah, on May 10, 1869, when the Central Pacific and Union Pacific rails were joined. Leland Stanford drove home the symbolic golden spike, activating a telegraph key that signaled "Done" to the nation.

The railroad opened the West to unprecedented growth and brought fabulous wealth to its builders. It also brought an outpouring of vituperation, which in some quarters has not ceased to this day. Of the riches that eventually led to the founding of Stanford University, Leland Stanford had this to say: "The wealth acquired by the projectors was entirely created wealth. The projectors alone had faith enough in the undertaking to support it; the stock at the completion of the road could scarcely have been sold by the bushel for ten cents, and it was held by the builders for the reason that nobody else would have it."

But opulence soon followed and a visible result was a richly-furnished forty-four-room mansion at Eighth and N Streets in Sacramento, to be followed by an even more stately house on Nob Hill in San Francisco, commanding a sweeping view of the bay and hills. Their new-found wealth contributed its share to the ostentation of the "Gilded Age," and Jane Stanford, now nearing her fiftieth year, accepted her role in it. Amid priceless originals in furniture and objets d'art, she played the gracious hostess to leaders in all walks of life from near and far. Despite their princely surroundings, what the Stanfords enjoyed most was the time they were able to spend alone, or with a few close friends, by the fireside.

Tangible evidence of Mr. Stanford's love and admiration for his wife were the splendid jewels he gave her and his many thoughtful, if at times lavish, acts of devotion. Bertha Berner, Mrs. Stanford's secretary and close companion, described a surprise birthday party Mr. Stanford gave his wife at Lake Como during one of their European trips:

In the morning Mrs. Stanford received an enameled box filled with unset topazes, golden and amethyst, but the unexpected came in the evening. Boatmen had been ordered to take them on the lake. Their barge was covered with garlands of flowers, and another, similarly decorated, carried musicians whose light-hearted songs floated softly over the water. As darkness fell, the hotel and hillside burst into a blaze of colored lighted. A feast was served in the large banquet hall for all who had taken part in the festivities. Later, in their rooms, they were again serenaded, the mellow voices and sweet melodies gradually fading away as the singers departed into the night.

The Stanfords' only child, Leland Jr., was born in Sacramento on May 14, 1868. Mother and father showed the joy of all new parents, excusably intensified by the late arrival of their heir after eighteen years of childless marriage. Nevertheless, Mr. Stanford could not spend much time with his son. His growing railroad empire kept him on the move from one key junction to another so that it was often difficult to locate him at a given moment, something Mrs. Stanford soon discovered.

Among Jane Stanford's earliest existing letters is one to her husband from an unidentified San Francisco hotel, where she was staying with her infant son and a domestic. As her letter intimates, the reason she brought her son to San Francisco during a spreading smallpox epidemic was to have him vaccinated by the family doctor. J.D.B. Stillman, a pioneer Sacramento physician and lifelong friend of the Stanfords, at the time was practicing in San Francisco. This first letter was followed by many from famous hotels the world over.

San Francisco; probably 1869

Dear Leland:

. . . I am tired of being here and thought on Saturday I would leave here today for home so as to surprise you and have things all nice and a good lunch ready, but Saturday night the baby seemed to be very worrisome and after twelve o'clock he was very fretful, crying at spells, just as he did that night you arrived at Helen's. Alice and I were up from two o'clock till seven trying everything to comfort him. I sent for the doctor and he advised a hot bath and a little gin sling, which quieted him, and he then slept three hours.

Yesterday morning after he had slept and we went to dress him we found most all his trouble had proceeded from his arm. His vaccination had taken and his arm is very sore today—he has spells of being cold and then again in a dripping perspiration. Doctor was in this morning and says he is taking it very severely all through his system, and at night he cried so that he no doubt felt just as a person does when coming down with smallpox. He had a splendid night last night and feels in good spirits. His arm is discharging considerably. Dr. Stillman said this morning he would rather I would not go up till Thursday or Friday, and the scab would come off. Crissa M. has a sore arm, too; hers took.

Dr. Blake met me in the hall this morning and asked me if he could see the baby. I brought him and Alice was just drying him from taking a bath. He said he was one of the finest children he ever saw, and "he was as fine as they ever made them." He said he had heard he was a

13

very remarkably fine child but he was more; he was so well made and handsome.

I went up to see Sister Frances this morning and thank her for her kindness. I was charmed with her and she seemed to be so much pleased that I called. She said, are you going to remain in the city long? I said I thought of returning very soon. She said, I would not stay here for the smallpox is terribly bad, much worse than the public generally is aware of, and it is constantly spreading, as people are very careless here. She says it is the very worst type that is raging here, the black smallpox, and that they have more knowledge of it as the Sisters are among it all the time. She is a beautiful woman; I fell completely in love with her. She spoke in the highest terms of you; she has such regard for you.

Let me know what you are going to do—if you are coming here soon; if not, I will return this week. General Franchot* and son sit with us at table; he is very social and pleasant. They sail tomorrow morning.

Now, dear Leland, I will say good-bye. I was delighted to get your letter. I see so little of you nowadays, a letter is more dear than ever. I feel as though I had so much to tell you about your being so good to me, doing so much. I am so much occupied with baby I am afraid I don't do my duty to you when I do have you with me—but my heart is full of love running over with the feelings I have for you, my blessed husband. I am not half good enough. I would like to be perfect that you might think me the best of wives. I shall be glad when we can be together all the time. I feel so lonesome, even here in the hotel. I miss you all the time.

With many kisses and a heart full of love,

Affectionately, your Jane
Baby sends lots of kisses.

At the bottom of the page is a scrawl with Mrs. Stanford's comment: "The baby's love mark; he did it with pen in hand."

---

* Washington lobbyist for the Central Pacific Railroad.

4

"Our boy was taken from us."

———◆———

*L*ELAND GREW UP an energetic, unspoiled lad. His parents thought a place in the country, within comfortable driving distance of San Francisco, would benefit the whole family. A farm thirty miles down the San Francisco Peninsula was purchased in 1876. It was watched over by a sentinel *Sequoia sempervirens* standing tall on the bank of San Francisquito Creek. Silently, through the centuries this stately guardian had watched the races come and go: Indians, conquistadores, padres, and now the latest breed with its strange devices and restless energy. This unusual tree, one trunk of which still stands, inspired the Stanfords to name their place Palo Alto Farm.

Vineyards, orchards, and a stock farm appeared, with a race track and sleek horses. A delighted young Leland joined the workers in the vineyards, at the stables and track, and in good season galloped across the fields and over the distant hills. He had an inquiring mind and everything possible was done to prepare him eventually to take over his father's vast affairs. A bent for languages and collecting historical memorabilia was encouraged and led to travel abroad.

During an extended European journey with her twelve-year-old son, Mrs. Stanford wrote colorful accounts of their travels and gave intimate little glimpses of young Leland's developing mind and lively interest in all that they saw and did. When Mr. Stanford was unable to join them as expected, Mrs. Stanford became homesick and resolved never again to be separated so long from her husband.

Brussels, November 17, 1880

Dear Leland:

Thinking you may possibly be detained and not get off as soon as you hoped, I will write a few lines from here and direct again to the Windsor Hotel. I wrote you a few days ago from Amsterdam, Holland. I stopped two days at Antwerp; from there I telegraphed you. I left there day before yesterday; it is only one hour from there here. It is not agreeable traveling now for it rains all the time. The week we were in Berlin the sun did not shine out but one day—and we have not been cheered with its presence since, but I have persevered in spite of wind and weather to take in all I could of this part of the world.

I get very tired but I make it a rule to be in bed at nine and I never rise till nine—at Berlin, Amsterdam, and Antwerp I felt quite vigorous and comfortably well. Saw all I could in the short time—but here I have had to rest. I was worn out and must have taken a little cold, although I am so enveloped in red flannel that even you would admit that at last I was sensibly dressed. We suffer no more in the cars from cold for they are now more comfortably heated.

From Dresden thus far I have traveled second class, as I did not want to be separated from Christine and George and did not care to pay first class fare for them. I have done just as well and better than I did before, for George goes before and by giving a fee to the gendarme secures the coupé to ourselves. From Dresden I forwarded all my trunks to Paris and I had reduced them at Hamburg to two, and since have only my valise—so you see at last I have learned how to travel comfortably. When we arrive at a station we have only these few small packages we can pick up, put in a carriage, and drive immediately to the hotel and secure a room before anyone else arrives. I always take one of the hotels Baedeker's guide book recommends and have as a general thing been pleased.

This is a beautiful city. I went out for two hours yesterday in the rain, taking Leland and going to the public picture gallery. Leland is quite adept at picking out the gems. We returned at one o'clock and went into the restaurant to get a little luncheon. It is very gorgeously gilded and painted and we were the only persons in at the time. He looked toward the desk, which was arranged something like a pulpit with books lying on the top; I had not noticed it yet. He said, "Mama, look at the recording angel." I looked around at the paintings—he said, no, there in the desk. I then saw sitting in this desk a young lady writing. He then said she will have to write faster than that to record all the deeds that men do on this earth. He is constantly getting off such odd sayings that he quite startles me sometimes. Here everyone speaks French, so now he begins as naturally to use it as if he had always spoken it—he astonishes me.

This morning he and George have gone to the Nature Museum, the Botanical Garden, to home at two. He is very anxious to go to Waterloo to the old battlefield. He was to have gone today with George but it is raining too hard. It is only twelve miles from here; trains go every hour. He felt very badly when he awoke and found it raining. He read up about the battle last eve. I sent and got a book, and the first thing on waking he said he had dreamed of finding bullets in the ground and he wanted to go and stand on the very spot where Wellington had stood. And another bright thing he said, "Mama it is not what you see there but it is what you take there that makes it interesting. Otherwise it would not be anything but a wheat field perhaps." I think Leland is far ahead of his years in good sense.

I will enclose a clipping from yesterday's London *Times*—an article about the C.P.R.R. I thought it might escape you and you ought to know who this writer is, evidently a Tom Scott* man.

I am trying here to rest and to allow Leland to go to Waterloo. The next day will go to Paris, leaving here at nine, arriving at three in the afternoon. I long to get there to my letters and perhaps a telegram telling me you have started for this side. I shall go to the Meurice Hotel but only till I look around and then settle. . . .

Affectionately, your wife
J.L. Stanford

Four months later Mr. Stanford had not yet started for Europe. Mrs. Stanford wrote to him from Italy:

Naples; March 16, 1881

My dear Leland:

. . . We left Rome day before yesterday (Tuesday). On Monday pre-

---

* Prominent Eastern railroad man and unsuccessful contender against the Central and Southern Pacific for the right to build a transcontinental line by the southern route.

vious we had much to enjoy. Hooker & Co., Bankers, had invited us to a balcony in a friend's house to see the King review the troops, it being his birthday, but before it was time to leave at half past nine we also received a note from Bishop Vaughn saying at twelve we would be presented to the Pope.* We also heard, just as we were about to leave, the report of the assassination of the Czar of Russia. His two youngest sons were in Rome and had been telegraphed for to return immediately. Mr. Grant of the firm and consul of our country came to escort us, and we had a fine view of the review. The Queen did not come out as was anticipated because of the news and her nervousness. The King, too, it was said, was quite nervous, as I should think he might be, as he is not a high standard of a man and the feeling between royalty and the church is bitter. But the parade came, the streets alive with people, the flags flying. The King rode a horse so like Onward it could be mistaken for him, and the next horse the same color and like Ned. Leland counted all the companies and footed up only 5,000.

At half past eleven we left, returned to the hotel to doff our bonnets and put on black lace veils; the dress one is obliged to wear must all be black. Miss Small from New York went with us to the review but not to the presentation. Leland took a half dozen rosaries to be blest and to give away. The whole thing made Clara supremely happy. We went up a good many steps to a private room in the Vatican, the Pope's guard dressed in beautiful costumes of yellow and black guarding the stairs. After waiting awhile in an anteroom where we left our wraps, we were ushered by valets dressed in crimson satin and velvet into an inner room where we found about 200 seated, all dressed in the black costume, black veils, the guards in full-dress white cravats—many looked like noblemen and ladies. We had to wait nearly an hour but the room was so beautiful—marble, mosaics, and frescoes—and the people themselves all interested me so much the time did not seem long. At last a chamberlain came and took all the miniatures from each, and soon after the Pope appeared—tall, thin, white as marble, dressed in white nacreous dress with a wide watered-ribbon sash round his waist—surrounded by six or seven chamberlains and guards.

He came slowly down the side of the room, saying a few words to each, laying his hands on their heads to bless them. An officer preceded him, asking the names and then announcing them quietly to the Pope. He soon reached us. The officer recognized Clara and said quietly to the

* Leo XIII, Pope 1878–1903; opened Vatican archives to scholars and constantly strove for peace.

Pope, *particularly*. So he halted behind Clara, laid his hand on my head and said, I give you the blessings of your heart. He then took my hand; his was like ice. On the third finger he had on his ring of sapphires and diamonds—that has been worn by all the Popes dead—and been kissed by so many. Next came Leland and I was quite amused to see Leland put the Pope's hand to his mouth and kiss the ring as all the others did. We staid awhile longer but not till he was entirely through as it was late and the room too cold without wraps. Leland said he shook so he could not first keep his teeth from chattering, but as the Pope reached him he was as cool as anyone. Clara was too happy to eat or sleep.

Tuesday we left at four and had a weary, hard ride till eleven o'clock. The car jolted so badly, the seat was so hard that, had it not been for the interest we felt looking at the country we passed, we would have been very exhausted. But all our attention was absorbed in the setting and oh, how beautifully strange this country is. As night came—and the beautiful silvery moon was full—it seemed as if we were in another world. The wind blew quite hard, but still the sky was clear and even crisp and like a night at home when the cold is so intense the sleigh runners squeak over the snow. Still, it was not cold and Leland said, "Mama, it seems to me this wind blowing past the moss has polished it so brightly—is the cause of it being so bright." We had the sea on one side and on the other the soft looking mountains and hills—green and dotted with quaint old castles perched almost at their tips overlooking the plain and the beautiful sea.

At last we saw the grand old mountain of Vesuvius—only its outline—but we neared it and discovered the red light issuing and the clouds of smoke. Leland was wild with interest. I have read a good deal to him about Rome and Naples—also the last days of Pompeii—aloud. We had written for rooms at the Hotel Bristol as Mr. Mills staid here. It is perched highest on the hillside overlooking Naples and on to Vesuvius. But we do not stay here in spite of its wonderful fascinations. Such a night as we had—clear, not a cloud, and we watched the great silvery moon in the blue sky as it rose from behind Vesuvius at eight o'clock last eve. The red light from the peak was in strong contrast. The moon rose and cast its rays of silver on the sea, over the housetops and palaces and the streets and houses below us and on our hotel. It was well worth all the anxiety and fatigue I have had about coming here.

I went out yesterday afternoon—Leland, George, Christine, and I— to the museum and spent two of the most interesting hours I have known since I came on this side. Oh, if you can only come to Rome and here I would not feel badly about the other places left out. You must see this old world. You cannot conceive anything like it on earth. This city is beautiful to me—and so strange—so beautifully located. The soft skies and the climate remind me of dear California, and the aspect of the country, too. But how young we are compared to this. There are 700 [?] inhabitants in this city and I saw more magnificent establishments, fine houses, liveried servants than I have seen anywhere; and then in great contrast the little donkeys carrying the panniers, with a woman between, and the peasants and native Neapolitans singing, playing—it is a study and pleasing. But I dare not stay here; there is so much typhoid fever among the visitors. So we leave at four today, go to Castellammare, one hour by rail and near Vesuvius. Will go to Vesuvius and Pompeii from there and return quickly to Rome, rest ten days and go to Florence, where we only rest, remain there about a week and then go on to Milan and Venice. I hope before I leave Florence to hear you are on the way.

Leland has just come. He has been on board a Russian dhow man-of-war. He is begging me to go to the Island of Capri but I cannot consent. I am anxious to get out of Italy now that it is quite warm so far south. Have just received your letter from Bremen, sent on, dated February 22nd. You are not sure of getting away early. I feel so disappointed. . . . I have a tutor in view, a teacher in the Anglo-American college at Nice. He speaks French well and teaches English to the boys. He came to see me twice and I hoped to be better decided but did not succeed; I take him only on trial. Leland speaks German and French quite well—uses it always with George, who is the best servant I have had around me; not a fault to find in him.

With love ever from your wife,
Jane L. Stanford

Rome, March 28, 1881

My dear Leland:

Today I expected to leave Rome for Florence—had coupé engaged and also rooms at the Hotel de la Velle in Florence—but have been prevented by the sickness of Leland. He showed on Wednesday, the day after our return here, that he had taken cold, but I thought with care and my old homeopathic remedies he would be all right in a few days, but Thursday night he had so much fever I sent for Dr. Valerie. He feared at first that he was going to have some kind of fever, but it has resulted in quite a severe attack of bronchitis. He is up this afternoon and the doctor assures me that with care he will be better and able to go on our journey by Thursday or Friday. I shall feel greatly relieved when we are safely away. I have had such a dread of Rome . . . but I argued with myself that it was only a morbid condition of my mind in consequence of not being well—and I must not yield to it.

I am now leaving without seeing half. The Palace of the Caesars—I have not seen the ruins inside; Leland went with Mr. Forbs the lecturer. I was not well enough to go with them, and Leland was going to take me himself on Thursday so that he could leave out that part he thought was too hard for me and show me the frescoes of Livia's room and the golden horse of Nero. He has it all at his tongue's end. You will be surprised how much this trip has done for him. I feel very proud of him; he is wonderfully bright, far beyond his years. The doctor says he has a mind like a man—all intellect—and that is why he is so sensitive phys-ically. He is called the little "Augustus" here by the artists, for his head is so much like the bust of Augustus, and he has been to nearly all their studios, and I find he has quite an acquaintance among them. He came in just before he went away and said, "Mama, I have been into a sculptor's where I have seen four of the finest pieces ever made representing the four seasons." So I had to go with him the next day and look at them—at an Italian artist's named Botiulli—and they were lovely—all originals. So after a few days I went again, made an offer of $900 for the four with pedestals, and took them. You will be charmed with them. He has seen a picture that he wants me to buy but I am not going to get anything more here, but will talk over with you about some things I have seen.

I am so anxious now to get on to Paris, hoping you will have started by this time. I am so homesick I cannot eat or sleep, and I often think if it were not for the strong will I exercise over myself I would give up. Oh, how long the time has been. I have solemnly promised myself noth-ing shall ever take me from my home and you again, if we are all spared to reach there together. I shall be so thankful if we can meet again; how I will rest soul, body, and mind. I don't know, dear Leland, if all I have seen has for one moment reconciled me to this long separation. I have tried to write you cheerfully and not complain, for I know you had heavy burdens in business. But oh, how my heart has cried out when alone at night and how earnestly I have prayed that we might all be spared to meet again. I don't dare allow myself to take the cup of hope to my lips yet that you will be here within a few weeks, for you say so little in your letters to encourage me. Clara has to leave me the first of next month. She says she will try and contact the children to let her stay till the middle if she can. She does not want to leave me till you come, but I cannot wish her to do what I would not do myself. I shall ever love and bless her for her goodness to me. . . .

I have read with great interest Secretary Black's address at the meeting in New York. I should think he was a sorehead. I did not like him in Paris; he was too good a Democrat. I wish Charles Adams would censure him; he knows more about railroad matters than most as he studied it long—and found it was too much for him. I wish you were out of all the railroads and could settle down to a more peaceful life. We would have something more hopeful to look forward to in the future than now, for the conservative spirit is spreading itself to such an extent that even men like Judge Black are in favor of dividing the spoils of the rich.

Now good-bye; my next will be from Florence.

From your wife,
Jane L. Stanford

The year 1884 found the whole Stanford family together in Italy. From Florence Mrs. Stanford wrote one of many letters to Timothy Hopkins, foster son of Mark Hopkins, and his wife, May. She first thanked them for a handkerchief case they had sent her, but the letter quickly took on a troubled tone. Leland Jr. was seriously ill, yet the doctor had not thought ominously so. She also spoke of her own and Mr. Stanford's poor health during the past two years, now thankfully improved, and ended on a happier note.

Florence, February 25, 1884

My very dear young friends, Tim and May:

To tell you how pleased I feel to know that you both give me kind thoughts is a pleasant duty. On our arrival here four days ago a package met my eye addressed to me, and when the lovely muchoir case and sweet note were handed me I felt that amid all the dark clouds that surrounded us there was one with a silver lining. Accept my tenderest love for this token of love.

We came here from Rome with our darling boy quite ill. He had complained while we were at Athens and again at Naples; he was sick enough to be in bed for a few days. We hastened from this unhealthy city to Rome. He appeared for a few days better, but I doubted the propriety of staying in this city and persuaded Mr. Stanford to allow me to come on here, and had I delayed coming one day he could not have been moved. As it was we had to bring him in a saloon car, with a bed in it. A physician met me at the hotel and took charge of him immediately, and after two days he pronounced it a mild case of typhoid fever. We have been here five days, and Leland is nearly at the highest point. The doctor thinks he will be confined for four weeks, even under the most favorable circumstances.

Of course, dear friends, I am sorely troubled and the cup is full of sorrow, but I have had so much sickness and so much to distress me the past two years. I have turned for comfort to the giver of both good and evil and my faith has increased, and now again I turn to Him with entreaties to save to me my darling boy. It has been prayer that has restored and given me my eyesight, and prayer gave back the present health of Mr. Stanford. He is not his old self entirely—he has pains and aches and looks fully his sixty years—but we are thankful he is as well as he is.

We had fixed on the third of April for leaving Liverpool, but now all will depend on Leland's state of health. We have not given up hope of leaving at the time named. I have heard through my brother of the return to California of dear Mr. Hopkins and his kindness in taking with him my sister. I am surprised that she cared to go when we were not there, to have her with us.

I am pleased to know Mr. Moses has married and thank him for our card telling of the fact. Mr. Stanford joins me in sending warmest friendship for you both, and remember us kindly to your dear aunt, Mrs. Hopkins.

Ever your friend,
Jane L. Stanford

Then came tragedy. On March 13, 1884, this cablegram from Florence was delivered to Mrs. Mark Hopkins in San Francisco:

> OUR DARLING BOY WAS TAKEN FROM US THIS MORNING AFTER AN ILLNESS OF THREE WEEKS WITH TYPHOID FEVER. PRAY FOR US.
>
> LELAND AND JANE STANFORD

5

Aftermath

THE UNEXPECTED DEATH of their only child was a tremendous blow
to the parents, but neither of them collapsed under the pressure of
grief. Leland was soon again immersed in business and politics and
within a year was to become United States Senator from California.
Jane, with fewer outside interests to divert her, stood bravely by the side
of her husband and her friends, and her letters show that she did not
let her own bereavement lessen her compassionate interest in the joys
and sorrows of others. And, of course, both Leland and Jane were de-
voting much time to planning the University they had decided to found
in their son's memory.

Much has been made by chroniclers of the Stanfords' grief. Mr. Stanford, as co-builder of the railroad that had linked fabulous California
to the rest of America, was a world figure and many of the things he said
or did were headlined around the globe. Every mile of the slow, sad
journey home from Florence was recorded in sentimental detail. Mr.
Stanford was not well, necessitating a stay in Paris, and they stopped

again in New York where business matters detained him. Press interviews and the germinating idea of an educational institution as a memorial to their son kept the Stanfords' private grief in the public eye.

It was during this period that Mrs. Stanford's interest in spiritualism was aroused. This was not unnatural. Belief in the possibility of the living communicating with the dead was widespread at the time and was given a certain amount of respectability through its acceptance by a number of highly placed persons, including some members of the clergy. It also brought an opportunity to charlatans. There seems little doubt that Mrs. Stanford became interested in the subject but was never convinced, and her own good sense and her husband's levelheadedness ended the matter.

The Stanfords' purported abnormal grief over the loss of their son and even the public hint that their minds had been disturbed were disposed of in an interview appearing in the *New York Herald*. Shortly before, almost a year to the day after his son's death, Mr. Stanford had taken the oath of office as U.S. Senator.

Herald Bureau, Washington, D.C., March 22, 1885

Senator Leland Stanford of California has, by his presence here and attention to his public duties in the Senate, quietly put down certain rumors which had been circulated through the press by ill-wishers that the loss of his son had, in a measure, unsettled his mind. No one who sees him or speaks with him or with Mrs. Stanford will have a doubt that both of them bear a very grievous blow with fortitude and self-possession, and that neither of them is so engrossed by a great grief as to justify the ill-natured and injurious reports which have been circulated about them. . . .

[Mr. Stanford told the correspondent,] "Mrs. Stanford and I have determined to devote a large part of our estate to public and, I hope, beneficent purposes. We want to do this while we are alive—to administer upon our own estate. I do not care to talk to you of the details of our design. They are getting worked out slowly and are not ready to be spoken of. But I wish to say this: I have seen a number of large estates intended for public and beneficent use wasted by litigation and, in effect, divided among contending lawyers. When I see these false reports industriously circulated about our 'monomania,' our devotion to 'spiritualism,' etc., I seem to see the train laying

25

and the way preparing for unscrupulous men to dispute, after my death, my competence to do that for the people of California and for the youth of that State which I want to do. I see the possibility of another great estate going, not where its owners wish it to go—to public and good uses—but to some lawyers. I am made uneasy lest a purpose which lies near my heart and my wife's may be defeated by greedy and unscrupulous men. You can see that this is not pleasant to either of us. That is the chief reason why I now speak to you in contradiction of false reports."

Mrs. Stanford's return to normal life is confirmed by her private correspondence. From Washington she wrote to Mrs. Timothy Hopkins:

Washington, D.C., January 29, 1886

My dear friend May:

A longer time has elapsed than I intended before writing you. My thoughts have gone so often back to dear Menlo* and traveled through your grounds, your sweet house, also through the lovely grounds of our friend and neighbor, Mrs. Flood, and through our own dear place, I am there in thought more than anywhere else, for there is no dearer place here on earth to us.

My sister is still here with us but will leave within a few days for California. I hope she will not be detained on her trip. I dread to have her leave me for the house will seem more lonely to me without her. Mr. Stanford is devoted to the Senate Chamber—is always in his seat at the opening and rarely leaves till the Senate adjourns. He seems to adapt himself to the extra cares with the same calm poise as he ever has in the past to new duties. We have thus far declined all social attentions. They are carried on to such a vast extent I wonder how the recipients live through such unceasing dissipation. Mr. Stanford accepted an invitation to a dinner of Mr. Dolph's to meet the Pacific Coast delegation. Today Mr. Stanford issued invitations to the coast delegation, fourteen in number, to dine with us on the 8th of February.

I received yesterday a welcome letter from your aunt. I was glad she kept us fresh in her memory; we can't spare our place in the hearts of our friends at our age—we hold them precious.

The storms have been very severe with you; we have read the papers with interest concerning them. The winter here has been unlike many

* Menlo Park adjoined the Palo Alto Farm.

26

in its snowfalls being severe. We have had our sleigh out four times, an unusual pleasure for Washingtonians. It storms today, snow and rain falling, but we, Anna and I, have concluded to go and hear Tossa play on the piano. He gives a public concert this afternoon. I hope, dear May, you received in safety the toilet set sent you when I visited New York during the holidays. It struck me as being your color and it was new in style, and I thought you would like it.

Remember me most kindly to dear Tim. I love to think I can address him lovingly. He has won me by his kindness always to Mr. Stanford and myself—and you, too, dear May.

Jane L. Stanford

Other letters to May deal with commonplaces and news of mutual friends. After an especially severe winter in Washington Jane told May that she and Leland were looking forward with impatience to getting back to their home and to Palo Alto. "That is such a dear, sacred spot fraught with such tender loving memories. The birds sing more sweetly there, and the trees and flowers are so much more beautiful."

When she learned that May was expecting a child, Mrs. Stanford put aside her own loss to express happiness for her friend: "I will send my poor petitions to the dear Father to be near and attend you through your coming event, which will bring to your loved hearts a child of your own." In due course a congratulatory telegram was sent to the Timothy Hopkinses on the safe arrival of a daughter. Jane Stanford grew to love Lydia Hopkins as she had her parents and never failed to mention her in the letters that were to continue through the years.

In 1888 the Stanfords were grieved to learn of the death of Charles Crocker. "It seems very sad to contemplate the changes that have occurred in the railroad associations with which we have so long been connected," Mrs. Stanford wrote. "Only Mr. Huntington and my husband are left here of the original number."

On another occasion Mrs. Stanford apologized to May for not writing in person because for two weeks her eyes had been so painful that she had even been obliged to give up reading her "precious book—Thomas à Kempis." This was a great deprivation for she was accustomed to reading the work of this great fifteenth century German ecclesiastic for an hour before retiring. Eye trouble plagued Mrs. Stanford from time to time and makes even more remarkable the vast amount of writing and reading she accomplished. Nevertheless, she was able to say at that time that both she and the Senator were enjoying better health than they had in the previous winter, adding: "Mr. Stanford surprises me with his ability to endure, and discharge the duties devolving upon him."

A year later Mrs. Stanford tells May of having sent gifts to Lydia Hopkins and her niece, Jennie Lathrop: "I send today a doll and outfit for the blessed child, Lydia. It seemed to me so attractive and I could fancy how she will enjoy the carriage, the cradle, and trunk. I send to our Jennie all she can enjoy at Christmas time."

Jennie Lathrop, the daughter of Mrs. Stanford's brother, Charles G. Lathrop, was destined to come under her care for a time. The child's mother, foreseeing her own death, had asked and obtained her sister-in-law's promise to supervise the child's upbringing. The first indication that the pledge was being fulfilled came in a letter to May Hopkins on October 30, 1892: "I have Jennie with me and she is a sunbeam, and, after I get used to having her ask numerous questions and her never ceasing activity, I shall take it more quietly than I now do. I have stopped her school going and have a governess to teach her at home."

Jane Stanford's guardianship of her niece began shortly before Mr. Stanford's death and continued through the difficult years that followed. In contemplating those trying times, she thought it advisable to inform Dr. Jordan of the status of Jennie's relationship to her in case any question should arise in later years. This she did in a letter from New York in November 1897.

"When I told my dear husband the request that had been made by Jennie's mother," she wrote, "he was most decided in his objections to my assuming such a responsibility, first because of my poor health, and because of the great cares I had already to bear, and because of some misunderstanding that might follow were I to assume the care. Some might feel it was adoption, which we both felt could never be, and we both felt that our hearts' best love had been given, never to be replaced by any other love for any but our own dear son."

Mrs. Stanford persuaded her unmarried sister, Anna M. Lathrop, to assume the care of Jennie, but the sister died when Jennie was seven and Mrs. Stanford took up the responsibility.

"To the best of my ability I have discharged my duty to this motherless child and I have the heartfelt satisfaction of knowing she loves me dearly," Mrs. Stanford wrote, by that time having cared for Jennie for six years. "She knows full well her true position—that she has not been adopted by me and never can be. . . .

"I make this explicit explanation in this letter to you that you may hold it sacred, and if—after my eyes are closed to life here, hands are folded, and my work finished—the subject should be discussed whether or not Jennie S. Lathrop had been adopted, you can use this letter and defend me.

"I hope and pray there will be no need to ever produce it, but I have learned by very sad experiences the greed for gain tempts beyond the ability to resist. . . ."

6

Founding the University

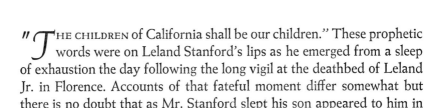

"THE CHILDREN of California shall be our children." These prophetic words were on Leland Stanford's lips as he emerged from a sleep of exhaustion the day following the long vigil at the deathbed of Leland Jr. in Florence. Accounts of that fateful moment differ somewhat but there is no doubt that as Mr. Stanford slept his son appeared to him in a dream and urged him not to despair of life but to "live for humanity."

"How I wish I could remember all he said to me in that dream," Leland told Jane years later in a conversation she recorded in her journal. "I know I resolved from that moment to build the University, and we both from that night resolved on this."

Even while their boy was alive, the family had in mind spending a substantial amount of their vast fortune for charitable and educational purposes. Howsoever it was motivated, there seems little doubt that the quotation about the children of California becoming their children originated with Leland Stanford and that Jane concurred heartily in the idea the words conveyed.

Planning the University, in which Jane Stanford took an active and equal part with her husband, occupied every spare moment. Senator Stanford had the self-confidence born of eminent achievement in other fields, but he wisely approached this new undertaking by first seeking the advice of leading authorities in the realm of education. Even before returning to San Francisco after Leland's death, the parents remained in the East long enough to visit Cornell, Yale, Harvard, Massachusetts Institute of Technology, and perhaps others.

While they were conferring with President Charles W. Eliot of Harvard the question came up of the cost of so ambitious a project as creating a great university from scratch. Eliot's considered reply was that it would take a minimum of $5 million. Leland, detecting a flicker of concern on his wife's face, gave her a smile and said he thought they could manage it.

Eliot may have had some qualms about the Senator attempting a project so far afield from his previous accomplishments and suggested they might give thought to adding to the endowments of established institutions, but that is not what the Stanfords had in mind. The more they considered, the more they visualized something new, something different—an institution that would profit from the lessons of the past, but also would be structured along new lines to meet the challenges of a new world they clearly saw approaching. At first they were determined that their university would break from the mold of classical learning and offer "practical education," but as their thoughts matured they conceived an institution that would combine professional training with the cultural arts.

Many changes had occurred in the San Francisco scene and in themselves since Leland had taken Jane's arm thirty years before to help her step from the deck of the *Independence* onto the planks of the Embarcadero. But whatever their mingled thoughts might have been at a particular moment on the 14th day of November, 1885, they were interrupted by the arrival of their guests; and the study of the Stanford mansion on Nob Hill, with its sweeping view of the city, bay, and distant hills, was soon filled with the easy conversation of long-standing friends. On that occasion, however, there was a more serious purpose for the gathering than that of a pleasant social hour. When their guests had been seated and the hum of conversation ceased, Creed Haymond, Senator Stanford's attorney, produced an artistically engrossed parchment and began reading aloud: "We, Leland Stanford and Jane Lathrop

31

Stanford, husband and wife, grantors . . . desiring . . . endowing . . . Leland Stanford Junior University . . . of high degree."

The even voice spoke on in legal language to rapt listeners, twenty-four of whom were named Trustees. Nothing quite like this had happened before; its scope and meaning were difficult to grasp. The Stanfords' vision reached far beyond the horizons of their day. "This Grant," the document read, "shall be liberally construed, and always with a view to effect the objects and promote the purposes of the grantors, as herein expressed." The breadth of the Stanfords' outlook was evident in the articles of endowment, which were in the nature of a constitution for the government and guidance of the Board of Trustees "in a general manner, not in detail." They hoped the institution would endure through long ages and were well aware that provisions regarding details of management, "however wise they may be at present, might prove to be mischievous under conditions which may arise in the future."

The object of the institution was to qualify its students for "direct usefulness in life" and to advance the "cultivation and enlargement of the mind." Its purpose: "To promote the public welfare by exercising an influence in behalf of humanity and civilization, teaching the blessings of liberty regulated by law, and inculcating love and reverence for the great principles of government as derived from the inalienable rights of man to life, liberty, and the pursuit of happiness." Its nonsectarian nature and the rights of both sexes to equal facilities and advantages were stressed, and the duties of its president and mode of operation of the University defined. The grantors retained control of the property and execution of the trust during their lives or the life of either survivor and also the right to alter, amend, or modify the terms and conditions of the grant.

When the reading and discussion had finished, the Board organized and elected Judge Lorenzo Sawyer its president. Senator Stanford formally delivered the deed, which the Trustees accepted by subscribing to its solemn duties—and Leland Stanford Junior University was founded!

Twenty long months had passed since the death of Leland Stanford Jr. in Florence during what had begun as a grand tour to acquaint the youth with the art and culture of the Old World. Through those trying months the parents' vision of a memorial to their son had assumed definite form. The University they contemplated now had a constitution and a name, but much remained to be done. As yet it had no buildings, no president, no faculty, no students. Six more years were to pass before a little band of Argonauts—faculty and students—opened wide the gates to the newest seat of learning in the New World among the oaks on the Palo Alto Farm.

General Francis A. Walker, president of the Massachusetts Institute of Technology, became the Stanfords' close friend and advisor. He recommended the prominent landscape architect Frederick Law Olmsted and Charles Allerton Coolidge of a well-known Boston architectural firm. Under the close scrutiny of Senator and Mrs. Stanford, they chose the University site and designed its buildings and grounds. The cornerstone was laid on May 14, 1887, the anniversary of Leland Jr.'s birth.

The Romanesque style, with its arcades and quadrangles, and the arboretum were the result of long hours of study and discussion. Happily, the architecture did not follow academic tradition but blended perfectly with the place and spirit of its surroundings. Stanford stood unique among the universities of the world. On the land where Gaspar de Portola camped on the way to discovery of San Francisco Bay and Junipero Serra trod the footpath that is now El Camino Real, arose the sandstone buildings, the red-tiled roofs, and cool arcades, symbols of a romantic heritage.

Obtaining the right president for the University was of the utmost importance. The Stanfords had long given thought to the sort of leader they wanted. He had to be a scholar, yet sympathetic with their by now well-formed progressive ideas on education. General Walker met all the requirements but he did not wish to leave his prestigious position before completing his goals for M.I.T. They next turned to another friend, Andrew D. White, who had put his innovative educational ideas into practice as president of Cornell. But he did not care to take on a new and untried venture in far away California. However, he had a good suggestion; the Stanfords should interview a former student of his, David Starr Jordan, the president of Indiana University, who had all the attributes they were looking for. The advice was immediately followed. Stanford and Jordan, so different in their chosen spheres, took to each other at once; their broad views on education coincided, their wives approved, and so David Starr Jordan left his secure and pleasant post in Indiana to head an institution that was in large part still only a dream. "With open eyes I have dared it,/And suffer no regret," he quoted.

On the 1st day of October, 1891, the opening ceremony was held in the Inner Quadrangle, which was decorated with California's finest greens and flowers. A colorful throng had gathered. In the forefront some 500 men and women students were seated in the sturdy frontier Douglas chairs to be used next day in their classrooms.

In the emotionally charged atmosphere, with Mrs. Stanford at his side, Senator Stanford addressed the students as a father might speak to his own sons and daughters on the threshold of their independence: "Remember that life is, above all practical; that you are here to fit yourself for a useful career; also, that learning should not only make you wise in the arts and sciences, but should fully develop your moral and religious natures."

President Jordan told of the aims of the University and several notables gave their good wishes. One talk expected by Senator Stanford was not given. The reason for this was disclosed six years later by Mrs. Stanford in a letter to Dr. Jordan.

San Francisco; May 24, 1897

Kind friend:

At the time of the opening of the University Mr. Stanford urged me to write something that I would read myself to the students. I complied with his request but when the time came my heart grew faint at such an ordeal and I could not bring my mind to face such an audience and read this address. Mr. Stanford was very much disappointed. I put the article away and did not remember that I had kept it until today on looking over a trunk of old letters I found it, and send it to you that you may read it and from it you can gather what my feelings were in regard to the work my husband and I were so much interested in.

I gave it to Mr. Stanford to read at the time, and he, as you will see, inserted a few words. Those were the only changes made in it, and I send it to you Simon pure.

Your friend,
Jane L. Stanford

Enclosed was the following address:

My husband has expressed the wish that I would address a few words to the students today. Perhaps it is befitting that I should do so, for since the first conception of this work Mr. Stanford and myself have been in unison and we have not only conferred together earnestly and deeply, but we have made this work a subject of deep and earnest prayer. We fully realize our own weakness and our inability to accomplish anything by ourselves. We are not deserving of praise for what we have done; we are merely following out a great plan that was conceived by one far

34

greater than ourselves, our Heavenly Father, and we are but lowly instruments in His loving hands.

Our hearts have been more deeply interested in this work than you can conceive. It was born in sorrow but has now become a great joy to our hearts. While Mr. Stanford has dilated on book education, I desire to impress upon the minds of each one of these students, both male and female, that we have at heart and very closely the hope that you will each strive to place before yourselves a high moral standard; that you will resolve to go forth from these classrooms determined in the future to be leaders with high aims and pure standards; and live such lives that it will be said of you that you are true to the best you know. I hope your lives will be truly earnest, not in the sense of going forth to acquire great wealth and great names; but to be conscientious workers, to be helpful to others, to send cheer and goodwill to those who need lifting up, and always follow the Golden Rule, "to do unto others as you would have others do unto you." ...

I am also anxious that these young men should treat the young ladies who have entered this institution with the greatest deference; that they will be helpful in aiding and cheering them in their ambition for a thorough education. We have started you both on the same equality and we hope for the best results. ...

Perhaps it will not be improper for me to say to these young men and women who have gathered here as students that this day is held by us to be one of the most sacred in our lives. We thought it a sacred day when we laid the cornerstone of this institution, and how often we have wondered if it would be our Heavenly Father's will to allow us to remain on earth to witness its inauguration. His tender loving heart has seen fit to spare us to take part with you this day. A great sense of thankfulness pervades my being that He willed it thus, and I deem it proper I should give public testimony of my gratitude.

Our hearts go out to you in a peculiar manner. I think that we both feel a personal and individual interest in each one of you; in fact it seems to me that you have become a part of our lives. Our hearts have yearned for a work which might rouse our interest in the life of the young and in this field our hearts are filled almost to overflowing with deepest interest. While we are permitted to remain in this life we shall watch closely your efforts to improve your opportunities and closely follow the results when you go forth to battle with the world. ... There is only one failure for you and that is not to be true to the best you know. Always be gentle in manner, resolute in purpose, and you will develop characters on which others can depend; and you can safely dispense with the more brilliant qualities if you can be depended upon for truthfulness, honesty of purpose; and each example of a good student will reach out and have an undying influence.

One who has passed away from earth life has said, "Kind words and liberal estimates and generous acknowledgments and ready appreciation, unselfish delight in the excellence of others—these are the best signs of a large intellect and a noble spirit. To be true, to be loving is the secret of Christian growth."

I hope each one of you will hold up this ideal before you and then you will go forth as missionaries into the world. This is what we wish, what we hope, and what we pray for.

Jane L. Stanford

Not read as expected as I did not have the courage that opening day of the University—so important in our lives. [J.L.S. *October 1891*]

Since that opening day Stanford University has sent more than 100,000 alumni as "missionaries into the world." The number of students has grown from 500 to more than 11,000. The faculty, now 1,000 strong, counts seven Nobel Laureates in its number. The twelve original Inner Quad buildings are ringed by libraries, classrooms, laboratories, dormitories, and playing fields. The University which Senator and Mrs. Stanford dedicated with such high hopes has become one of the most important centers of learning in the world.

7

A Woman Alone

————◆————

SHORTLY AFTER the University opened, Senator and Mrs. Stanford
returned to Washington. Time was never idle on their hands. Mrs.
Stanford was a much sought after hostess and at no time did her Washington calling list number less than 1,000. Her formal dinners and re-
ceptions were the epitome of elegance. Tablecloths and serviettes with
lace motif inserts of finest Belgian needlework, gold service plates, taste-
fully arranged flowers in silver vases, and an epergne overflowing with
California fruits presented a connoisseur's delight.

Meanwhile at Palo Alto the University began its course in a burst of
youthful enthusiasm. It had been the founders' aim that Stanford University be different than existing ones; and so it was, though possibly
not to the extent they had envisioned. Nevertheless, Stanford was in
the forefront of the changes taking place in higher education during the
latter part of the nineteenth century—from the rigid course of study of
the classical period, with its class distinctions, toward more practical
courses and the ideas of equal opportunity and freedom of choice. Stan-

ford University helped lead the way by setting up new guideposts with new conventions and customs in an idyllic setting far removed from the trappings of tradition.

The founders watched the development of their University with approbation and visions of its future growth. Whenever they visited the campus, they were particularly pleased when the students came to their home, as they often did, to greet them with songs and cheers, sometimes followed by conversation and refreshments.

In an effort to improve the Senator's continuing poor health, the Stanfords went to a French spa in the summer of 1892 and so were unable to attend the institution's first commencement. However, a letter to Dr. and Mrs. Jordan from Jane Stanford and the pages from her journal which follow show the Stanfords' intense interest in everything pertaining to the University.

Aix-les-Bains; July 13, 1892

Dr. and Mrs. Jordan:

Ever since the accounts of the first commencement at dear Palo Alto reached us I have had it on my mind to write you. I want you to know we are deeply interested in all and everything pertaining to the success of the undertaking so dear to our hearts. We received a pamphlet containing the order of exercises, and other interesting data. I observed all was simple and met the approval of friends, also the public. I am pleased to know many of the graduating students will return; it gives evidence of entire satisfaction that they return. We feel it will take time to put affairs on a firm basis; wonders have been done in so short a time; even our fondest hopes have been more than realized. As we look over the field now, our minds are more quieted and our anxieties and fears less. It seems wonderful things have worked so smoothly.

I feel that the Doctor is a tower of strength. When we look back to this time last year, how much there was to do and then to be ready to care for 500 when we thought 250 would be a goodly number to start with, we should all feel satisfied and be thankful for the help all have received from the unseen power who is ever ready and willing to aid His children on Earth.

We noted what was written in regard to the malicious attack on Professor Barnes—it did not alarm us in the least. Those things are almost everyday occurrences and treating it with contemptuous silence is the only course to pursue.

We received several copies of the students' handbook, which I think is very useful and also interesting. It gives one so much insight into affairs generally. I notice with great satisfaction there is a strong element of Christianity and it is all spontaneous, which makes it genuine.

I know you are anxious to hear about Mr. Stanford's health, as we came here to benefit him. Tomorrow will be a month since we arrived and he commenced the cure. It has been rather severe and generally makes the patient weak, but the reaction comes after a week or more in the high cool atmosphere of the Swiss Alps. We shall start day after tomorrow. Lake Geneva is but three hours by rail from here. We stay there but two days, then on to Bern for two days, then to Battenberg on the Lake of Thun. There we will take the rest and after-cure and stay until we tire of the place. We will tour around but little for it is against the doctor's orders. The middle of August we may possibly come back here for the second cure that is on the slate, but sometimes Mr. Stanford breaks the slate—it depends on his improvement. I feel quite satisfied with the result and can plainly see the benefit the rest and freedom from care have been to him, although care follows him in respect to his private affairs—and he would not want to feel he was not needed and his usefulness over, so it is well to be missed and to let him know it.

We have been made sad by the serious condition of my sister's health. I hoped ere this she would be able to go into the country and be strengthened by the balmy air of San Jose, but all my news of her is rather depressing. Mr. Nash* was stricken down with a severe hemorrhage the night we arrived in London. He is still there but is now sitting up and has taken a drive and hopes to start homeward the last of this week or next. Mr. Lathrop, my brother, remained with him, so we have been here alone except for our servants. We have missed Mr. Nash very much, especially Mr. Stanford as he has depended on him for his shorthand and his letter writing. I have offered my services but I find I am accepted only in a case of emergency.

The heat here is debilitating, the air full of humidity, and we hold up dear Palo Alto before us with its charming climate, its beautiful scenery, its azure blue sky; and, since it is peopled with so many boys and girls and learned professors and their interesting families, it is more attractive than it was eight years ago when desolation seemed written on the face of all there.

* Herbert C. Nash had been Leland Jr.'s tutor, then secretary and friend of the Stanfords, and later University librarian.

I am glad to know you, the Doctor, and your dear children keep well. Health means happiness and health gives a rainbow hue to life wherever one may be. Mr. Stanford joins me in all I have written. . . .

Yours sincerely,

J.L. Stanford

The following pages from Jane Stanford's journal are the only indication that she had kept such a record. She had given them to Dr. Jordan at his request in 1897 and told him at the time that she had kept a diary since her first visit to Europe in 1881 and, while going over it in the previous weeks, had destroyed all except these two entries:

Bern, Switzerland, July 19, 1892

Leland and I have had a talk quite unusual and I feel like making a note of it.

After dinner I sat down at the piano and played some of my old-time pieces. Leland was lying on the sofa; he had felt weak all day and was quiet and thoughtful. I thought my playing would soothe and distract his thoughts from his condition of health. He had said once during the afternoon to me, "I have never felt as weak on my legs as I do today, and when I walked out did not know but my legs would give out entirely."

The day has been damp and cold and rainy most of the time. We arrived here yesterday afternoon on our way to Battenberg on Lake of Thun.

I had been very depressed all day by seeing Leland so discouraged. After lunch he took a nap and then went out for a little walk and it was then he must have felt so weak on his legs. After his return he rested awhile and then proposed a ride. We went around the place and then to the hill where the view was so beautiful and which I enjoyed so much twelve years ago with my darling boy. When we reached the hill it was so changed in all its surroundings I did not recognize the spot and was thankful, for I did not know as I could hide my feelings from Leland and I knew I must be brave for his sake. We returned to our hotel, had our dinner, and I was still struggling to be cheerful for his sake when I seated myself to play. After a while he called me to sit down by him. He took my hand in his and said, "I have been thinking a good deal about our schools. I want such men as Franklin and Morse turned out from them, men that will go out as missionaries to work among humanity.

"A gentleman who called upon me at Geneva said he thought there

40

was too much education being done. I asked him if he thought he had been educated too much. How shortsighted, how little he has thought of the question.

"I want to live to build up a grand institution, make the grounds attractive, and those halls not finicky but substantial, and I want the boys taught to think. When I was a boy I read such books as *Francis Marion* written by Major Harny. Marion went down in the cave to kill a bear. He wanted the darkey to go, but he was afraid. But Francis Marion had a rope put around his waist, was let down in the cave, and killed the bear. I read this and I appreciated his feeling, for I rarely ever felt fear.

"I remember reading how Franklin made his kite with its iron points and then attached a key and raised it when a thunderstorm was coming on. And he touched his knuckles to the key and the sparks came from it, and he started this which now is applied electricity. So it has gone on; Morse perfected it, and what would the Indian think to have had the light come as it did tonight while we were at dinner without any visible means. Look at it. You cannot see the force that makes it, but it exists. And I want these scholars to be taught that they can go on and know the finite, can never reach the infinite, but can approach it.

"If all goes well, I hope to put better buildings than are there for homes.

"I want to better humanity. I used to teach our boy to always be sure and so conduct himself as to respect himself, then he would be pretty sure to be happy. I think he never forgot that. He was a truthful boy, too, and did not care to read books that were not true, and it is very important what books boys read. I had my whole life influenced by the books I read.

"I wish I could remember all that came to me in that dream the night Leland went away. I do not remember all, but I know it was a great help to me. It made all the difference in the world—something to live for and make that University a place to send boys out to do missionary work.

"And you, too, are as much interested as I am and have done all you could, and, if you live, can go on with it."

Jane L. Stanford

Aix-les-Bains; September 4, 1892

We arrived here for the second cure for Leland Wednesday evening about five. I think there has been a gradual improvement in my husband's health but I do not approve this second cure—it is too weakening, but Dr. Blanch approved it.

41

This morning when I first awoke I looked over at my husband's bed and found him awake. I rose and approached his bed. As I did so he said, "I have been lying here thinking about our boy and how sad that he was taken away from us, but how much worse it would have been if we never had had him."

I then stepped closer to the side of his bed and said he has opened the gates of Heaven to us, and we would not have him back, for now we will be with him soon, and there longer with him than if he had staid here and reached your age. And with the temptations that would have surrounded him, with all you would have left to burden his young life in the way of care and property, knowing nothing of the deceits of life, would not you and I be far more unhappy there, even if Heaven were ours to enjoy, than we are now, for now we know he is safe from all harm, his soul is free from sin, and he is acceptable to our Lord Jesus. He is ours to go to—Heaven is dearer because he dwells there.

He said nothing for a few moments but after a while remarked, "How I wish I could remember all he said to me in that dream. I know I resolved from that moment to build the University, and we both from that night resolved on this, but I have been thinking how it was we decided on Palo Alto, and we have never for one moment regretted it. On the contrary, it has been everything to live for."

Seeing he was through, I said it was all marked out from the beginning that he should come to us, stay the time he did, and then go to the Giver, and he did his work as was intended and it has saved our souls, for we love the Savior. Leland smiled and said, "Yes, I believe it."

Yesterday, September 3rd, my dear sister has been in the life eternal one month, and I said to my dear husband how much more she knows than she did a month ago. My boy may be her teacher.

These talks always comforted our hearts, made us brave to go on to the end.

"It is not all of life to live, nor all of death to die."
Jane L. Stanford

Jane Stanford and the Senator were able to attend the University's second commencement in 1893, but his steps were uncertain as he was helped to the platform. The ceremony was simple. "The dullest thing I ever saw," said a newspaper reporter. Outwardly drab it undoubtedly was, but inwardly satisfying for its participants. Attendance was small, many students having left right after finals to take summer jobs. The professors who came to say a few words to their major scholars strolled in wearing their classroom clothes. There were no caps or gowns or multicolored hoods to catch the eye. The only bit of brightness here and there was furnished by the women.

The short ceremony over, Mr. Stanford exchanged a few words with Dr. Jordan and others about him and, again supported, he and Mrs. Stanford returned to their carriage. A few days later the Senator spent a pleasant evening with his old partner, Captain N.T. Smith, reminiscing about their early storekeeping days in the gold country. Returning home he told his wife he felt weary and retired to his room. Putting out his light, he called to her: "Jennie, I just want to tell you that I love you." That night Stanford died quietly in his sleep. The date was June 21, 1893, and he was sixty-nine years old.

Mrs. Stanford withdrew briefly midst the fragments of her shattered world. Apparently she did little writing other than short acknowledgements of letters of condolence, but there is one poignant note in the Stanford University Archives addressed to Bishop and Mrs. Newman, friends from Washington, D.C. "Sitting here in this dear room alone, *his* library, I can only speak a few words," she wrote. "My heart is too full for utterance. I ask myself each day how it can be I live with this great, overwhelming sorrow upon me, never for any time away from my thoughts—only when I sleep and the awakening is so dreadful. At first I say, is it not a dreadful dream, but no, it is too true and again I face the truth."

Dr. Jordan expressed the feeling of the campus:

Palo Alto, June 25, 1893

My dear friend:

I have felt impelled to send a word to you—a word that may be of help and consolation—though all human words must sound weak and cold in the presence of such great sorrow.

Ever since I first met Mr. Stanford I have had a steadily growing realization of the unique simplicity, purity, and majesty of his character. He was a real king among men, the noblest product of our American democracy from which the real kings of man may come.

With all our sorrow for Mr. Stanford's death—and with all our regret for the possibilities for good which a greater fullness of years might have brought him—we have the feeling that his life has been as rounded and complete and successful as human life may be—that insofar as his work is unfinished, others can take it up and no part of his strength need be wasted. . . .

43

As for us who are teachers in the University, I may speak for all of them, I am sure, in saying that we have no other ambition than to help in carrying out his plans and yours—so long as, in God's mercy, our help can be useful in the work. When we can no longer help we shall be content to stand aside that others strong and wiser may do what we have dreamed of doing.

I am very sincerely yours,
David S. Jordan

Strengthened by support from the campus community and convinced that Providence had chosen her for the task, she resolved to finish building and chart the course of the institution she and Leland had worked together to create. She could scarcely have foreseen how difficult this role would be or the hidden strength that would enable her to fulfill it so abundantly.

In a handwritten document prepared several years later for the laying of the cornerstone of the Thomas Welton Stanford Library on the Outer Quadrangle, Mrs. Stanford disclosed the gamut of her emotions during the short period immediately after her husband's death, when she had secluded herself from the outside world. With revealing openness she confessed her initial self-pity, followed by remorse, and finally the revelation and her vow to finish the work Providence had entrusted to her:

Palo Alto, November 1, 1898

Among the contents of the copper box which will be placed in the cornerstone of the Thomas Welton Stanford Library building tomorrow, the second day of November, I have put a crucifix which stands for my faith in Jesus, the crucified one—and I wish it perpetuated and interwoven with the erection of every structure on the campus. Thus far the crucifix has been placed with the Bible in each cornerstone— one in the quadrangle, one in the museum, and this in the library building.

Since the placing of the cornerstone in the museum building, very many experiences have come into my life. In 1893, June 21st, my dear husband was suddenly and unexpectedly called from earth life to the "Fair Beyond." There followed this dreadful sorrow, developments and experiences such as the world could not understand or believe. They are far beyond my wish or ability to portray. For a while I felt like one on a sinking ship on a tempestuous sea. . . . I shuddered and closed my eyes as I thought the ship would sink, but clung to God's promises to the helpless—the widow, the weary who wanted rest. I wanted to join my loved ones and was not afraid to *die*. I knew it would be gain to me.

Suddenly there loomed up before me the blessed work left to my care by my loved ones, and I felt that my course was cowardly. I was so impressed by the new light which dawned over me it brought the first tears to my eyes. I wept day and night in penitence. I had forgotten God, Jesus Christ, and the angel world that held all that was dearest and best to me. They all said, live—take care of your body—it is the only instrument given you to do the will of the Lord. I promised most solemnly to live for the work that I now saw was God's work, not mine. . . .

My husband's brother, Thomas Welton Stanford of Melbourne, Australia, to whom my dear husband had bequeathed $300,000, in the tenderest and most comforting words . . . wrote me how touched, how grateful, he felt that his brother had so generously remembered him; but knowing the condition of finances all over the world, knowing a little of the circumstances surrounding me, he could not accept the gift for himself and he now tendered the entire sum to me for my sole use to do with as I pleased. To this proposition I could not consent and made a new one to him, that I would accept half if he would take the other half and allow me to take the half I retained and build a library with it, calling it the Thomas Welton Stanford Library—his gift. To the latter he did not consent but expressed his regret that I did not apply it to myself. As I have no needs for self that have not been satisfied I feel it but just to him to use his generous gift for this purpose and thereby link this noble-hearted brother of my husband's to this institution, that it may be a testimonial of his sympathy, his heartfelt and sincere interest in the advancement of the work which is I trust, by the grace of God, to continue through ages to come. . . .

> Jane L. Stanford
> Wife of Leland Stanford,
> who passed to life immortal
> June 21st, 1893

8

A Challenge Accepted

———◦◉◦———

T HE WIFE WHO had lived long in the shadow of her famous husband emerged a lone woman of unsuspected perceptivity and will—and she needed it all. With the Senator's estate in probate, funds for operating the University were not immediately available, and to make things worse, the country was in a financial panic which bankrupted every major Western railroad save the Southern Pacific Company, which held the Central Pacific and allied lines. Cruelest of all, the government initiated a suit attempting to establish the estate's liability for $15,237,000 in railroad construction loans not yet due. While the suit was pending, the estate could not be distributed, and a decision favorable to the government would bring an end to the fruit of Senator and Mrs. Stanford's labor and dreams—Stanford University, its bright beginning, its hope, its promise, dashed beyond recall.

The aging widow began her newest duty with one resolve indelibly etched in her mind. The University would be kept open, nothing would swerve her from this purpose. When told point-blank "The University

46

must be closed!" by a grim-visaged gathering of San Francisco's leading attorneys and bankers, she was undismayed. "Do you think I believe that my husband's carefully laid plans can wholly miscarry?" she replied. They would learn what one determined woman could do.

The probate court allowed her $10,000 monthly, about the amount she had been spending on her household, but this must now also provide professors' salaries and other expenses of the University and stock farm. Well! She had been a frugal manager before and could be one again. Domestics were cut from seventeen to one cook, one maid, and a secretary whose salary was deferred for nearly a year. Six strings of choice pearls were sold at a sacrifice. All moneys over $350 a month for personal expense (about the equivalent of a professor's salary) were given to President Jordan to dispense in whatsoever way he thought best, but Mrs. Stanford kept a sharp eye and taut rein overall.

Although Mrs. Stanford had been a full and eager partner in planning the University, she had kept in the background and had not concerned herself with finances or the management of the Stanford personal properties, which were not then on a paying basis. No endowment for the University had been set, and the buildings, grounds, equipment, salaries, and other expenses had been personally provided for by Mr. Stanford. Thus, at the age of sixty-five, Mrs. Stanford was faced with the gargantuan task of providing the institution with funds to meet all of its needs.

The $10,000 allotted to the widow by the court was not automatically doled out but had to be realized from assets that were constantly decreasing in value in a panic market. "People think that Governor Stanford left me a very rich woman," she said. "I thought so myself, but it now seems that I was left a legacy of debt, trouble, and worry; am without money and cannot realize on securities. The railroad company has taken advantage of my reserve and silence. They hold the keys of the treasury and unlock it for their own uses. I am so poor my own self that I cannot this year give anything to charity."

Nevertheless, in a statement to the press she declared it her solemn duty to carry out the great work which had been so successfully inaugurated; she was thoroughly conversant with the details of the Senator's plans and wishes; her life would be devoted to completing the task. President Jordan was overjoyed though not surprised by her decision, but there was some questioning among the faculty as to how well she could be counted upon to carry out her resolve. The government suit and the clamor of some legatees, even a few from the Stanford and

Lathrop families, for prompt payment of the inheritance the Senator had so generously provided only added to her burden.

Despite the amenities and unquestioned authority that great wealth had brought her previously, when suddenly faced with adversity her excellent mind and basic qualities of orderliness and propriety stood her in good stead. Unswerving loyalty to her husband's aims and ideals is evident in everything she said and did; and lastly, faith in a divine Providence enabled her to surmount every obstacle and become, in Dr. Branner's words, "The real founder and the greatest benefactor of Stanford University."

In many ways those troubled years were Stanford's finest. Everyone—faculty, student, worker—was united in a common purpose. The University took on new meaning. The red-tiled roofs, the Quad, the Row, the Chapel, and, yes, the unpretentious post office (favorite meeting place and communications center) became symbols of fortitude, faith, and good cheer. Salaries were cut with few complaints or thoughts of leaving. A dealer furnished coal free for the University power plant; merchants gave unlimited credit to the needy, and as time went on, the patches on professors' clothes became a hallmark of quality. Dr. Jordan retained his natural optimism and the students, with faith in their leaders and the excitement of fresh outlets in learning and living, remained cheerful and unconcerned.

Face-to-face exchanges between Jane Stanford and other protagonists in the dramatic events of Stanford University's early years were numerous and many were later recorded. For communication over distances beyond the reach of her voice, she used the written word. Telephones were a rarity. The only one on the campus when the University opened was at Escondite Cottage, President Jordan's home. There is no evidence that she ever rang that number. Many of her missives traveled no greater distance than from her campus home to the office of Dr. Jordan. Most of her letters to Dr. Jordan are addressed with the salutation, "Dear friend" or "Kind friend," and close with "Your friend," to which on occasion the adjectives "earnest," "sincere," or "grateful" are added. Something of her mood may be gleaned from their usage.

Mrs. Stanford was absent from the immediate scene from time to time for reasons of business, health, or rest—though in the first years following her husband's death little was accomplished in the latter regard—but she was never out of touch. Her letters are postmarked Palo Alto, San Francisco, Sissons (a favorite Northern California mountain retreat), other points in California, New York, Washington, and localities abroad. Jane L. Stanford's pen draws a picture of Stanford University's first years—its trials, its triumphs, its hopes, its prayers—which has no equal.

Once, in need of a few days away from the scene of her trials, she took her private car to Siskiyou in southern Oregon, there to refresh body and spirit in mountain air and forest shade. Urgently called back, she was dismayed to find that a railroad strike blocked all means of return. The strikers were bitter and violent; in some sections federal troops were called to protect life and property.

Though they were poles apart in their social outlook, Mrs. Stanford did not hesitate to carry her problem directly to Eugene V. Debs, head of the American Railroad Union and perennial Socialist candidate for President of the United States. During a forty-eight-hour period tapping telegraph keys sped these messages back and forth along the right of way:

To Southern Pacific officials from Mrs. Stanford, July 1, 1894

HAVE JUST ARRIVED AT SISSONS. THE BURNING OF THE TRESTLE PREVENTS MY GOING FARTHER AT PRESENT. WILL GO TO DUNS-MUIR FROM HERE BY CARRIAGE AND AS SOON AS POSSIBLE WOULD LIKE A CAR AND ENGINE AND PROCEED TO SAN FRANCISCO. I HAVE NO FEAR WHATEVER TO CONTINUE MY JOURNEY. I FIND THE STRIKERS ARE ANXIOUS TO SIGNIFY THEIR ALLEGIANCE TO MY HUSBAND'S MEMORY BY CARRYING ME SAFELY TO SAN FRAN-CISCO. I HAVE THIS ASSURANCE FROM THEM.

To Mrs. Stanford from S.P. official, July 1, 1894

THE MEN WHO ARE ON A STRIKE HAVE ASKED ME TO SAY TO YOU THAT THEY DO NOT THINK IT SAFE NOW FOR YOU TO GO FAR AND WOULD ADVISE YOU TO REMAIN AT SISSONS UNTIL WE CAN FIND OUT HOW OUR TRACK IS. THINGS ARE NOW LOOKING BAD. ONE OF OUR TRESTLES MILE WEST OF MONTAGUE WAS BURNED THIS MORNING. THIS TRESTLE IS OVER 900 FEET LONG. IF THINGS QUIET DOWN AND OUR ROADBED IS IN GOOD ORDER I WILL SEE IF WE CANNOT TRANSFER YOU TOMORROW.

To Eugene V. Debs, Chicago, from Mrs. Stanford, July 1, 1894

THE TRAINMEN OFFERED THEIR SERVICES TO TAKE ME SAFELY HOME. THEY HAVE KINDLY BROUGHT ME IN MY PRIVATE CAR WITH TWO SERVANTS AS FAR AS SISSONS. THEY HAVE JUST TEL-EGRAPHED ME THAT, WHILE THEY ARE STILL WILLING TO TAKE

ME, DESIRE THAT I OBTAIN YOUR PERMISSION AND SANCTION.
IT IS ALMOST AN ABSOLUTE NECESSITY THAT I SHOULD BE IN
SAN FRANCISCO ON TUESDAY, JULY 3RD, TO ATTEND TO IMPOR-
TANT BUSINESS. MOST OF THE MEN IN YOUR ORGANIZATION ARE
OLD, DEVOTED FRIENDS OF MY HUSBAND, AND IT IS TO TESTIFY
THEIR RESPECT FOR HIS MEMORY THAT THEY ARE ANXIOUS TO
TAKE ME SAFELY OVER THE ROAD TO MY HOME. I WILL BE
READY TO LEAVE DUNSMUIR MONDAY MORNING AT EIGHT
O'CLOCK AND BE TAKEN TO SACRAMENTO. THE NEXT DAY PRO-
CEED TO SAN FRANCISCO TRAVELING ONLY BY DAYLIGHT. KINDLY
ANSWER TO DUNSMUIR AND OBLIGE.

To Mrs. Stanford from Eugene V. Debs, July 2, 1894
THE TRAINMEN WILL HAUL YOUR CAR TO ITS DESTINATION ON
PRESENTATION OF THIS TELEGRAM. IF THERE SHOULD BE ANY
FURTHER INTERRUPTION PLEASE ADVISE ME AND I WILL BE GLAD
TO ASSIST YOU IN ANY WAY IN MY POWER IN SAFELY REACHING
YOUR DESTINATION.

To Eugene V. Debs from Mrs. Stanford, July 2, 1894
I APPRECIATE MORE THAN I CAN EXPRESS YOUR KIND ACT. I AC-
CEPT IT AS A TRIBUTE AND MARK OF ESTEEM TO THE MEMORY
OF MY HUSBAND, WHO FOR TWENTY-FIVE YEARS WAS HELD IN
VENERATION BY ALL OF HIS RAILROAD EMPLOYEES. IT WOULD
HAVE PLEASED YOU TO HAVE SEEN THE JOY IN THE FACES OF
THE REPRESENTATIVES OF YOUR ORGANIZATION HERE TO CARRY
OUT YOUR SANCTION OF THEIR DESIRE.

9

United States of America
vs.
Jane L. Stanford, Executrix

———◆———

"THE UNIVERSITY will be open to the poor as well as the rich," Mr. Stanford had told an interviewer during the planning stage, "and I hope to bring the cost of living, with an abundance of good wholesome food, and a variety, so low that people of very moderate means can there obtain an education." But this did not mean there would be no charge: "Certainly there will be a charge for tuition. I do not believe that anyone should have something for nothing. It is one of the first objects of the school to teach that labor is respectable and honorable, and that idleness is not."

However, before the University opened in 1891, the Senator decided against tuition—and there was none until 1920. But there was a nominal registration fee and one of Dr. Jordan's early requests to Mrs. Stanford was that five dollars each semester be added to the fees of the freshman students. He pointed out that he had had to curtail some work, especially in mechanical engineering, and that professors' salaries were still scaled down some six percent below their nominal figures.

He hastened to add, however, that he was not asking to increase them. The answer came promptly by telegraph:

Los Angeles, February 23, 1895

My husband's main object in establishing University was to give full education to the students. I would defeat this by consenting to your proposition of additional charges and cannot consent to it. We must keep on doing as we have for the past year and a half.

When the University opened, its library contained about 3,000 books. Two years later, through gift and purchase, the total was 15,000. In 1895 a valuable and much desired collection, the Hildebrand Library, consisting of some 4,000 volumes and 1,000 pamphlets on German philology and early literature, was obtained in a manner not to Mrs. Stanford's liking. Again a telegram to Dr. Jordan succinctly expressed her view:

San Francisco, March 11, 1895

I cannot consent to purchase that German library by soliciting subscriptions from my friends and the Trustees of the Leland Stanford Jr. University. It is very distasteful to me and must be abandoned.

The matter lingered on, however. A year later it was the subject of a letter to Dr. Jordan.

San Francisco, April 15, 1896

Dear friend:

Your letter of the 13th was read with a feeling of sadness and disappointment. I went so closely into particulars regarding my financial condition, really took you into my confidence almost to an unwanted degree, thinking that I would in that way secure your protection from the harassing and tormenting applications for the use of money, which always hurt me to refuse. When I repeated to you the conversation between Professor Miller and myself, you kindly said, "Had I known Professor Miller was going to apply to you for aid in buying this library, I would not have permitted it." I consider it very indelicate on Professor Miller's part to have intimated that I could guarantee the refunding of this sum from the legacy of Mr. Thomas W. Stanford, when that fund is available. I find I shall have to be very guarded hereafter in my conversation as regards money affairs.

It has pained me very much that the professors think they have the liberty to apply to any of the Trustees for money. These Trustees were not appointed with the idea that they would ever be called upon to aid in supporting or helping the University in any financial way. When they were solicited to aid in purchasing the library which Professor Flügel was so anxious to secure for the University I did all I could to prevent it, although I knew full well what an advantage it would be to the University to secure it. It was deeply mortifying to me that I was not able to purchase it myself, but it was far more mortifying to me that the Trustees were solicited, and did come forward, and, with the aid of the professors, make the purchase. I do not think it is wise to allow such liberties on the part of the professors, for there are always opportunities to buy if there is money to purchase with, and we will always have to practice economy in purchasing for the future. And I think, my dear friend, that you should be consulted in all purchases.

I hope that Mr. Hopkins will never again be applied to to spend money for the Stanford University. Already his generosity and his goodness of heart have been abused, and it was this feeling that prompted me to send the telegram which I did last night for I do not want this money borrowed of anyone, nor do I wish it begged of anyone.

Your friend,
Mrs. Leland Stanford

The objectionable debt was eventually cleared by a successful fair, held in the Museum under the direction of Librarian Nash and Mrs. Jordan.

With the frequent irritations she was subjected to and the reality of her financial situation constantly before her, Mrs. Stanford began to falter in her brave resolve to keep the University open. The initiation in 1894 of the government suit—"United States of America vs. Jane L. Stanford, Executrix"—had been a severe blow. In a letter to her lawyer, Russell J. Wilson, from Sissons, where she had gone to collect her thoughts in the mountain solitude, Jane Stanford opened her mind and heart.

Sissons, March 30, 1895

Dear Sir:

I pen a few thoughts, which I submit for your consideration, and would like you to give me your opinion after they have been seriously considered.

The great calamity has overtaken me and is a great blow. We have worked unceasingly in a vain endeavor to avert its descent; it is all

53

plain to me now what must be done. If only I could comfort myself with the fact that this case is one in which the right will prevail, I would not have another moment's anxiety. It is not a question of right. It seems to me the question is which side will present the best legal talent, the most plausible approach to our country's executive. It is clearly a case of diplomacy. The fact of the injustice has been amply discussed, although people will continue to feel it their duty to express their regret and indignation. All I can say in reply, while the claim is unjust, I trust for a just settlement. I wish all action to be taken to be brought to my knowledge, and no one outside of myself to take action, as it is I and only I alone whom this concerns. Although not versed in law matters, my instinct will guide me.

There was a time when the thought of closing the University even for a short time was more than I could endure, but I have come to look upon it differently. To have those doors closed, students dispersed, would cause the state—the country—to realize more than ever just what was our desire to do for the benefit of others. You know how easily a good thing is accepted and taken for granted, but let that good thing be removed and great the effort to regain it.

When my husband passed from Earth life a friend said of him, "His conquests cost no tears, made no slaves, marred no lands. He conquered greed and sordid self and made all his own the portion of each aspiring youth of our land."

Those words are truly said, and if only the sentiment is remembered I have no fears. There is no need for me to tell you the story of my hard struggle to be brave, to be true to the very best impulse within me. You know much, but far from all. Only my Father in Heaven knows all I have suffered and endured since my husband was called from my side, to keep the doors of the University open. I fled to the mountains that I might find quiet and peace before committing this, my resolve, to paper.

This is not hastily done. It has cost me many sleepless nights—many tears. I lived, prayed to live for the good of this institution. It has ever been a work of love; is combined love for son and husband. I have maintained it since July 21st, 1893, in the greatest difficulty, making self-sacrifices that would make my husband weep, did he know it. I felt that my compensation would come when the trials and sorrows of life mortal were over, and I with my loved ones. I dreamed my Father God would lay his hands upon my head and tell me he had witnessed the struggle and for reward had given greater, richer blessings to my loved ones in Heaven, and we were now united, never more to be separated.

It seems to me Heaven is full of prayers for help to sustain this University. I have never cared for any portion of my husband's estate for purposes of self. I thought only of the good I might be able to do for the University. I tell you all this that you may know what it costs me to close its doors. I feel I have nothing to live for. I have a humane heart and it is already broken.

Excuse this long letter. I could not control myself to say all this face to face.

Your grateful friend,
Mrs. Leland Stanford

The change of scene and rest evidently restored Mrs. Stanford's composure, for she did not take the step she had dreaded. Mr. Wilson must have reassured her, but her strongest support came from her brother, Charles G. Lathrop, the institution's business manager and treasurer: "Jennie, you are not up against the wall yet. I advise you to keep the University open until you are." Its doors were never closed.

Mrs. Stanford was frequently worried about her health and had been considering a prolonged and relaxing trip; but, as she explained to Dr. Jordan, the pressure of her responsibilities outweighed all other considerations.

San Francisco, June 27, 1895

Dear friend:

I hasten to let you know I have decided not to go on the intended trip to England. I did feel I owed consideration to my health first, but I am doubtful about being satisfied with myself if I put such distance between myself and affairs which require constant watching. I will go to Vina for a few days and thereafter will take short trips, returning once a week to meet my coworkers and let them know I am here, heart and hand, to do my part in the work before us.

Your friend,
Mrs. Leland Stanford

10

Lessons in High Finance

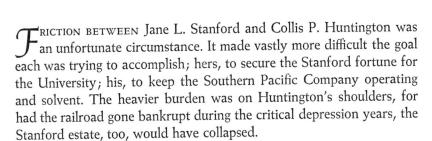

*F*RICTION BETWEEN Jane L. Stanford and Collis P. Huntington was an unfortunate circumstance. It made vastly more difficult the goal each was trying to accomplish; hers, to secure the Stanford fortune for the University; his, to keep the Southern Pacific Company operating and solvent. The heavier burden was on Huntington's shoulders, for had the railroad gone bankrupt during the critical depression years, the Stanford estate, too, would have collapsed.

An early dislike between Governor Stanford and Huntington, more evident on the part of the latter, had not prevented them from cooperating in building the Central Pacific Railroad. Each liked the wealth and power that great achievement brought; their differences were largely matters of temperament. Huntington was cold, calculating, aloof; Stanford warm, friendly, with a sincere desire to help his fellow man. The distrust continued between Huntington and Stanford's widow.

Jane Stanford made it clear from the beginning that she was going to make her own decisions.

Mr. C.P. Huntington
Dear Sir:

Your favor of July 10th, 1894, delayed because of interruption in the mails, was received by me several days ago. Replying thereto, I will say that after consultation with my attorneys, Messrs. Spencer and Wilson & Wilson, we have come to the conclusion not to give any power of attorney either to yourself, General Hubbard, or Mr. Stillman, as suggested by you, and to add that I am unwilling to give any power of attorney to any other person whatever in the matter.

Respectfully,
Jane L. Stanford

The Pacific Improvement Company frequently mentioned in Mrs. Stanford's letters, in which Leland Stanford had held a one-fourth interest, was a valuable asset in his estate. It was a construction and finance pool with extensive real estate holdings in California and New York, as well as a depository for stocks and bonds of the Southern Pacific and other railroads, and was the source from which Senator Stanford had borrowed much of the money for the initial building of the University. Jane Stanford was the sole executrix of her husband's estate and her worries about financing the institution during the protracted government suit were compounded by the required liquidation of these debts and payment of legatees before money could become available for the University.

Huntington had managed to take the presidency of the Southern Pacific Company from Stanford in 1890. Mrs. Stanford had no confidence in Mr. Huntington's trusteeship of the railroad and the closely allied Pacific Improvement Company and believed that his policies were the cause of the increasing public clamor against the railroad. Contrariwise, Huntington considered some of Mrs. Stanford's decisions on railroad matters, in which she now shared a responsibility, as obstructive, and with ill-concealed annoyance he gave her a beginner's lesson in high finance.

New York, October 30, 1894

Dear Mrs. Stanford:

Mr. Douty has sent a telegram to Mr. Gates, which has come to me, that you refuse to sign the note to the Corn Exchange for $100,000 when we only owe them fifty thousand. Now you can readily see that when notes become due many of them have to be paid, and, of course, we have to borrow money to pay them. In the case of the Corn Exchange Bank, we owe them fifty thousand, and they said when it became due they would like to loan us a hundred thousand. Now, that is the way we have to borrow money—that is of people who want to loan us—and people who want their money, of course, we have to pay. Then we had to borrow money to pay the interest due the first of October which, of course, was new money.

It does seem to me, Mrs. Stanford, that you have known me and also General Hubbard and Mr. Stillman (although you have known them a less time) long enough to trust us. I never knew men more honorable in all their business dealings than Stillman and Hubbard, and I think you ought to feel confidence in our management of these financial details. We are doing no new things, but we must carry on our business, and can only do it successfully by doing it harmoniously as between the different interests. I have been disposed, and all of us are disposed, to stand by you in your own matters. You have money to raise sometime and we expect to help you if you need help; but you must go along with us, signing paper as we sign it, and trust us to do whatever we in our best judgment think ought to be done. There is no other way by which we can go forward, and, if we cannot together do this, then there is no other way but to part company.

I believe Governor Stanford never questioned my integrity or my ability to do the things we had to do, and I am disappointed that you should cavil about matters, as you seem to be doing, when it is so important to yourself and all of us that differences should not exist. I can only ascribe your feeling to the annoyances to which you must be subject, and I regret that they have to come; but it is even more to be regretted that you cannot feel like assisting the New York office to carry on the business that must be done, and which is vital to your interests, if it is to anyone's.

Yours very truly,
C.P. Huntington

Mrs. Stanford was not convinced and in the following letter to her attorney only agreed to vote for Huntington's continuance as president upon a promise that he would be asked to resign within the year.

San Francisco, April 4, 1895

Mr. Russell J. Wilson
Dear Sir:
Let me again assure you that under no consideration whatever would

I permit the vote to be cast in my name in favor of the president now at the head of the S.P. Railroad had not Mr. Stillman positively promised me that during the coming year he should be asked to resign his present position. He has also promised me the present obnoxious management of affairs here in California, which has so antagonized the whole state it has endangered the one-fourth interest left by my husband in properties here under the control of Mr. H.E. Huntington and Mr. Schwerin [several illegible words], be removed from controlling any interests of mine under their management during the coming year. I consider their management has endangered the interests left by my husband, which is one-fourth of the entire whole, to such an extent that I would be held responsible by the probate court and the legatees did I not protest and assert myself as to its future management.

If these promises are not complied with during the coming year, those interested with me in all those properties must be prepared to conduct their financial affairs without my assistance and the use of my name after the date named. I feel confident Mr. Stillman is a high minded and truly honorable gentleman and will live up to his promises. Consequently I put trust in him and allow you to vote today for C.P. Huntington, president of the S.P. Railroad—of which I had no intention until these assurances were received in your hearing, Judge Spencer's, George Crocker's and my brother, Charles G. Lathrop's.

Yours most respectfully,
Jane L. Stanford

Had Mrs. Stanford been able to get along with Mr. Huntington, she might have spared herself unnecessary worry. After all, he was the acknowledged financial genius among the four associates who had built the Central Pacific Railroad and eventually the Southern Pacific Company, the source of the wealth Mrs. Stanford was now trying to preserve for the University. Either she failed to recognize this or allowed prejudice to sway her, which was perhaps understandable under the circumstances. Huntington thought Stanford had been extravagant and had let his interest in politics, land, viticulture, and race horse breeding outweigh his good railroad sense. Wasting money on a university was the last straw. "Stanford's Circus," he called it. Stanford's widow was quite aware of Huntington's disdain and in return did not withhold her own feeling.

As president of the Southern Pacific, Huntington had considerable authority in managing the railroad assets which formed the bulk of the

Stanford estate. Jane Stanford's lack of good judgment in financial affairs, as Huntington viewed it, must have been a constant irritant to him and the members of the board and goes far to explain their sometimes caustic comments. Jane Stanford's undeniable skill in handling small but essential details at times prevented her from seeing the whole picture. Had she been able to, she might even have been given reassurance on the government suit, but this she looked upon as a matter of preserving her husband's integrity and honor, far more than one of merely saving dollars for the University.

She continued to be displeased with the way others were handling her business affairs. She was considerate but firm to a lesser official, N.K. Masten, financial agent of the railroad company: "I wish to inform you that hereafter I will not place my name upon any notes or obligations without being consulted in the matter. I allow no one to make any promises of this nature without my consent. I make an exception in this case as you appear to be an innocent party in the present affair."

In a letter to her attorneys Jane Stanford made a crucial decision which later added considerably to her woes.

San Francisco, April 16, 1895

Messrs. Wilson & Wilson
Dear Sirs:

After carefully thinking over the engagement of Judge Garber as associate counsel with yourselves in the government suit against the estate of my late husband, I have concluded it is best to have it managed entirely independent of the Southern Pacific Railroad and Pacific Improvement Companies. This decision renders it impossible for me to accept assistance from said companies. I feel obliged to pay all fees myself.

Yours respectfully,
Jane L. Stanford

In June of the same year, A.N. Towne, second vice-president and general manager of the Southern Pacific Company in San Francisco, wrote to T.E. Stillman, a New York attorney and director of the company, explaining why Mrs. Stanford was delaying a decision on a most important resolution before the board. "The object of this letter," Towne wrote, "is to explain that neither Mrs. Stanford, her brother, nor her attorney knew anything about this matter except through a casual remark of Col. Crocker's a day or so ago." As a result Towne had spent two hours trying to explain things to them and pacify them, but Mrs. Stanford was indignant and postponed her decision. He suggested that if in the future she were told things in advance, it would bring a more harmonious feeling all around.

Towne then wrote a long letter to Mrs. Stanford pleading for co-operation. Referring to the original associates, Stanford, Huntington, Crocker, and Hopkins, he said that they were inscribed in the financial and railroad history of the generation as "the great road builders of the world" and declared that no other coterie of men had done so much for the people at large as those four progressive builders. He attributed their success in no small measure to a unanimity of purpose. Differences of opinion were openly weighed and discussed but the final decision was always voted unanimously.

The point then at issue was whether the Central Pacific should remain under the single management of the Southern Pacific as the board fa-vored or be divided with perhaps great impairment of the value of Jane Stanford's own property. Her correspondence does not reveal her deci-sion, but whether she voted aye or nay, the roads remained united under the banner of the Southern Pacific, and the Central Pacific became a name in railroad history.

During prolonged absences Jane gave her brother, Charles G. Lathrop, full power to act in her behalf in all matters except those concerning the University faculty, which she entrusted solely to President Jordan. Even so, when a decision of major importance had to be made, Lathrop sought his sister's advice; in this instance an agreement for the purchase of stock by the Pacific Improvement Company:

Montreal, December 23, 1895

Messrs. Stillman and Hubbard
Gentlemen:

Mr. Lathrop informs me he declined during my absence to sign the agreement made between J.H. Roberts and C.E. Hooper of the City of Sacramento and the Pacific Improvement Co. for purchase of 1,800 shares of the capital stock of the Sacramento Transportation Co., repre-senting an investment in the neighborhood of $300,000.

He mailed to me a copy of the agreement presented to him to sign, saying if I authorized him to sign he would "cheerfully do so." His re-fusal to sign meets with my emphatic approval, and I have telegraphed him to this effect.

It was agreed, and I supposed thoroughly understood by all the prin-cipals of the P.I. Co., that they should not enter into any new enterprises or purchase any more property—in other words, not further encumber the P.I. Co., but aid in every way possible to liquidate and lessen its indebtedness.

As executrix of my late husband's estate, I decline to place my name on this agreement or any other paper not calculated to lessen the debts of the P.I. Co. I consider it my duty to place myself on record as having lived up to the meaning of our agreement. When my acts as executrix are investigated by others who have rights in my husband's estate my transactions shall not be open to criticism.

I do not wish to be considered an obstructionist or a hindrance to the vast business we are all interested in. I am following my own sense of honor and duty towards others who have rights in my husband's properties, and are trusting me to be just and faithful to the sacred trust reposed in me. . . .

Respectfully yours,
Jane L. Stanford

Meanwhile, the government suit against the Stanford estate, filed June 3, 1894, was languishing in the Circuit Court. The government was seeking $15,237,000 for the estate's share of the government construction loan made to the Central Pacific. This loan was secured by a mortgage given subsequent to an act of Congress of 1862, passed to aid in the construction of the Central Pacific and Union Pacific to save California and the Far West to the Union. The government feared that the railroad was not going to meet its debt when due a few years hence—an erroneous belief as it turned out since payment was made in full—and so filed the suit based on a California statute of stockholder's liability. The government claimed the rights to its benefits without being bound by the express statutory limitation of liability to three years.

The estate could not be settled while the suit was pending. A decision was urgent. Jane Stanford could no longer stand idly by. She summoned the only queenly luxury still hers to command—the rosewood paneled private car, "Stanford," which she had given her husband in happier days. Over the rails it sped for Washington where she was determined to seek the aid of President Cleveland. All she would ask would be for him, if possible, to speed consideration of this issue so vital to the life of the University.

It was not an easy thing for her to do. Though determined, Jane was by nature shy, and it was difficult for her to assume the role of suppliant. The pressing need, however, overcame her reticence and she obtained an interview with the President.

Grover Cleveland received Mrs. Stanford at the Executive Mansion and, after listening cordially to her plea, penned this note in his own hand to Attorney General Olney:

April 30, 1895

My dear Mr. Olney:

Mrs. Stanford has told me her story and wants very much to see you.

You will not find her at all unreasonable or troublesome. It will be a relief to her if she can see you and I hope you will give her the opportunity.

Yours truly,
Grover Cleveland

After her interview with Mr. Olney, he promptly wired the government counsel in California to push the suit in order that it might make the Supreme Court calendar in October.

Returning to the modest hotel in New York she now used instead of the Waldorf-Astoria, Mrs. Stanford expressed her gratitude:

New York, May 9, 1895

To the President of the United States
Hon. Grover Cleveland:

I would not be true to myself were I to leave unsaid the deep gratitude that fills my heart that you accorded to me so gracious and courteous a reception.

You made easy a hard and most painful task, for I had to step far beyond my natural womanly reserve and timidity to reach you and then to lay before you the inner struggle of my life to sustain the work so dear to the heart of my husband.

Since my visit to Washington I have decided to keep the doors of the University open another year, hoping and trusting in an all-wise God that it will go on as long as the State of California exists.

Your kind letter to Attorney General Olney secured for me a very kind and patient hearing, and he generously consented to do all in his power to hasten to a speedy termination the government suit against my husband's estate. I have implicit confidence in his promises and leave for home today with the great burden somewhat lightened.

I shall never cease to be grateful to you, my distinguished friend, for your kindness and, if the suit should be decided adversely, I will ever feel that in time of deep loneliness and distress you befriended me.

Your grateful friend,
Mrs. Leland Stanford

A similar but shorter note went to Attorney General Olney.

During her stopover in New York Mrs. Stanford received the following penned reply from Joseph H. Choate in answer to her request for an appointment: "Dear Madam: I was out when your note came. I will do myself the honor to call upon you at the 5th Avenue address at five o'clock tomorrow afternoon."

In the interview that followed Mrs. Stanford made a new friend in the person of Mr. Choate and secured his services to present the argument for the Stanford estate before the United States Supreme Court. Despite her belief in the justice of her cause and the efficacy of prayer, Jane Stanford's pragmatic good sense led her to seek the best possible talent. And so it came about that she engaged the man who was recognized as the leading lawyer and diplomat in the country to champion the Stanford cause.

11

As the Oak Tree in the Open Field

———◆———

*T*HE DECISION favoring the Stanford estate issued by Judge E.M. Ross in the Circuit Court in June 1895 was the first break in the storm clouds that had gathered over the University and brought an immediate message to Mrs. Stanford from ever optimistic President Jordan: "The good news from the court is received and we are all rejoicing. Accept our most hearty congratulations on the success of your cause and on the good omen of the future. God's errands never fail."

Mrs. Stanford's reply was restrained; she knew her ordeal was not yet over: "Dear friend: Accept my sincere thanks for your kind congratulations and sympathy. I dare not yet rejoice."

The full depth of her feeling was expressed in a letter to the presiding judge. Clearly, it was what she considered the vindication of her husband's honor that so aroused Jane Stanford's emotions.

San Francisco, June 1895

Honored Sir:

I would be untrue to my better self, false to my wifely, motherly nature were I to remain silent and not in a feeble way give expression to the feelings which surcharge my soul this holy Sabbath day.

More than all this I would be a recreant in my duty to my Heavenly Father and the Holy Family did I accept the blessing that has come from answered prayers and still remain silent.

God in His mercy ruled that a just and righteous judge should pronounce judgment and you have graciously done more for me than save millions; you have by this decision vindicated the honor of my husband, the father of my sainted son—which is more precious to me than untold gold.

My two years of care and sorrow have seemingly unfitted me to rejoice, but it has made me tender and sensitive to kindness and I shall ever be grateful to you for your righteous decision.

Yours most respectfully,
Mrs. Leland Stanford

A discordant note was thrust into an otherwise harmonious occasion by a newspaper account which had caught Mrs. Stanford's observing eye. According to the *San Francisco Call* of June 30, 1895, as soon as the campus had learned of Judge Ross's decision, the flag was raised and the little community abandoned itself to rejoicing. President Jordan was quoted as saying: "I regard the decision of Judge Ross as final. It is hardly possible it will be reversed. . . . Mrs. Stanford proposes to put the estate at the disposal of the University just as soon as the courts will allow her. When this is done we will turn our attention to library extension and classroom expansion; we will increase the laboratory facilities and make additions to the faculty. . . . The number of applicants will, no doubt, be largely increased, but the limit must remain at 1,200. We don't want an army. We prefer a small number, well organized and well equipped."

Dr. Jordan's reported enthusiasm was not shared by Mrs. Stanford.

San Francisco, July 1, 1895

Dear friend:

I enclose this clipping which I read in the Sunday *Call*. Please be more careful and not give any intimation of what I may do in the future, because the future to me looks very unpromising. This suit is far from having been decided. Mr. McKissick will bring it into the Court of Appeals and from there it will go to the Supreme Court. It may not be decided within a year, and even though it is decided, I know from the financial condition of the railroad company that I shall feel very reluctant to make any demands, except for what is absolutely necessary, and as for building and hiring more professors, I may not do that for several years.

If I am able to keep the University in the condition it is at present, I shall feel more than thankful; $15,000 a month is a great expenditure and exhausts my ingenuity and resources to such an extent that, had I not the University so close to my heart, I would relieve myself of this enormous burden and take rest and recreation for the next year. But I prefer to keep the good work going on in its present condition, and I am not promising myself anything further for the future until the skies are much brighter than they are now.

Please be very cautious what you say. This article has already had a very depressing effect. I have strenuously denied myself to all reporters as I do not think it safe to give them any information as to my future course.

Yours respectfully,
Mrs. Leland Stanford

To which Dr. Jordan hastened to reply:

Stanford University, July 1895

Dear friend:

I am very sorry that the interview in question has caused you more trouble. Most of this was not said by me but was filled up by the reporter whom I saw only for a moment.

I said that I did not think any court would reverse Judge Ross's decision, and that in any event the number of students would not be increased, our effort being to make the school effective rather than large. The part I have marked with a pen is not mine at all.

We all know that the legal condition is not changed, but everyone is greatly gratified to know that the judgment of Judge Ross is wholly against the government suit. . . .

I am very truly yours,
David S. Jordan

The warmth of Mrs. Stanford's reply to Col. C.F. Crocker, son of Mr. Stanford's late partner in the Central Pacific venture, is in contrast to the coolness she later developed toward him.

San Francisco, July 2, 1895

Col. C.F. Crocker
Kind friend:

Among the vast number of telegrams from the United States and Europe that have poured in upon me within the past few days nothing pleased me more than your beautifully expressed letter of congratulation and sympathy. You stand unique among my husband's associates as being the only one who has expressed sympathy and interest.

I have passed through such new, strange, and depressed experiences within the past two years, I am not able to rise above them and have not yet rejoiced. The curtain has not risen high enough yet to permit me to see the promising dawn of a better day. I have been almost a recluse; the world could not afford me diversion, my load of sorrow has been too deeply fastened upon my heart to ever be lifted from the influence. I have throughout it all endeavored to be just and honorable in the very highest sense of the word toward my husband's associates. I have been peculiarly situated; this government suit rendered it so. I do not feel certain it would end during the term of my life here on earth, and I deemed it a duty to those who come after me to not so obligate my husband's property, *which was not mine,* to an extent that would subject my actions to censure and bitter criticism. . . .

I mean to trust you and count on you as one whom I can call on in an emergency when others who should be true as my husband's associates fail me.

Gratefully yours,
Jane L. Stanford

From her Vina ranch in Northern California, where she had gone on her doctor's advice for a much needed rest, Jane Stanford answered the many congratulatory messages she had received and, as always, kept in touch with Dr. Jordan. "I hope and pray that the final decision will be as sure as the first. It means more to me than you or the world have dreamed, it means an unsullied untarnished name as a blessed heritage to the University. . . . God cannot but be touched by my constant pleading, and this first decision by Judge Ross makes me humble that I, so unworthy, should have received the smallest attention from one so tried by my lack of love for Him in years past and gone."

This is the first intimation that she had not always been as steadfast in her belief as was so manifest in later years and may help explain the subsequent intensity of her Christian faith.

A few weeks later Jane Stanford again addressed Dr. Jordan and enclosed a letter from Andrew D. White, president of Cornell, who had proposed Jordan for the presidency of Stanford and had since become a close friend and admirer of the Stanfords.

San Francisco Cal July
27th 1895 —
Mrs Timothy Hopkins
My dear May —
My trip home
was all one could   here and
have wished, The   velopes
drive from Toda   such an
Springs to the   uilding
we will never   indows —
forget — The grandure   kindly
of the mountain   dams, fr —
scenery, the luck   ms.
Jennie had finding   you
of Joseph Ellies,   high
our driver, all these   hope —
                             peace
and happiness —
Love to Lydia —
Ever Yours most
gratefully
Mrs Leland Stanford

With Leland Jr., three months.

Jane and Leland Stanford on wedding day.

Their mansion on San Francisco's Nob Hill was an area showplac

The Stanford home on the Palo Alto Farm.

Young Leland with his mother.

President David Starr Jordan.

The Library, before the 1906 Earthquake.

A view of the Chemistry Building and Museum from Outer Quad.

Dedication ceremonies in Inner Quad, October 1, 1891; Jane and Leland Stanford seated.

Collis P. Huntington.

The jewels Mrs. Stanford intended to sell.

"Palo Alto Spring," painted by Thomas Hill in 1878, includes a large number of the Stanford and Lathrop families. Jane Stanford is to the far left, with her mother, Mrs. Dyer Lathrop, seated next to her. Behind them is Mrs. Stanford's sister, Anna Marie Lathrop Hewes. To their right, Mrs. Elizabeth Phillips Stanford is seated next to her son, Senator Stanford. The artist is behind them, and to their right is Leland Jr.

"PALO ALTO SPRING," 1878, BY THOMAS

Memorial Church, in heart of Inner Quad.

A detail of the church interior.

ORD UNIVERSITY MUSEUM OF ART, STANFORD FAMILY COLLECTION.

Mrs. Stanford, center, on a visit to Egypt.

With Stanford alumni in Hawaii.

The Palo Alto Farm was noted for its racing horses.

Kind friend:

. . . I send a precious letter from Mr. Andrew White for you to read. I read it with a heart running over with various emotions. Mr. Stanford esteemed him so highly I could not but feel like asking God to let my loved ones in heaven know the contents of this letter. I prize this letter beyond my ability to express; it lifted up my soul from its heaviness. . . .

If you will kindly return Mr. White's letter I desire to file it away with many others of the same nature, and when our troubles are over all will be placed in your care for future reading by the students, a story for them when I have passed into peace that my heart longs for. I shall then be with my husband and my son. I know they count the days as they pass; each one brings us nearer together. This truth keeps me brave.

Yours sincerely,
Mrs. Leland Stanford

Dr. White's letter:

Ithaca, N.Y., July 13, 1895

Dear Mrs. Stanford:

It is long since I have been so deeply touched by anything which I have read in the newspaper as by an interview with yourself regarding the present condition of your noble university and your own relations to it.

And I have rarely rejoiced over any piece of news as much as over the decision of the United States Court in regard to the suit being brought against your estate. You have shown and are showing a spirit which does honor not only to American womanhood but to human nature. Long after we are both gone, centuries indeed afterwards, your conduct in all of this matter will be held up as a beautiful example to American men and women.

As to the suit, I have never had any doubt as to the ultimate result, and I believe that, like many things which seemed at the time calamities in the history of Cornell University, it will prove to be a blessing in disguise by making the friends and alumni and alumnae of the Stanford University even more devoted to it than they otherwise would be.

It seems in the order of nature that every good growth or great thing must cost pains and trouble, perhaps agony, before it can fully be brought into the light and made to do great work for humankind.

The University will be all the better for this storm, as the oak tree in the open field, exposed to all the blasts, sends forth its roots more widely and deeply than one which is protected.

I have just returned to America after my three years' absence in Russia and elsewhere in Europe, and find my hopes of American institutions of every sort, and especially of our better institutions of learning among which I especially include Stanford, vastly strengthened and increased. Never did their work seem to me more worthy, never were my hopes more sanguine regarding our educational system than at present. . . .

I remain, dear Mrs. Stanford, most respectfully and sincerely yours,

Andrew D. White

Dr. Jordan commented: "I return the good letter of President White, which I have read with great interest and pleasure. I am sure that everyone interested in higher education will feel as he does, when all the facts are known.

"Every effort to keep the University alive will count a thousand fold in the future. One great element in the earnestness of the student body has been their loyalty to you, when they have come to realize what you have done for them—in personal interest and sacrifice as well as in furnishing the means of education. I am sure you would be helped and strengthened if you could hear what the parents of our students are everywhere saying of you, and of the influence of the University. In my two weeks in Oregon and in Southern California I met very many of these parents, and their loyalty and enthusiasm was not less than that of the students. . . .

"I hope that you will let nothing lower your health and courage. I have the fullest faith in the ultimate future. This University is one this world cannot afford to lose and this world is too good to be willing to let it die."

Many who did not know Mrs. Stanford personally wrote to her. Her valiant battle to keep alive the young university in fabulous California aroused the admiration of the whole world.

12

Complete Victory

JUDGE ROSS'S DECISION, however welcome, did not free Jane Stanford to execute the bequests of her husband's will. In a document dated July 25, 1895, San Francisco, California, she made a full report to the legatees to acquaint them with the provisions of the will and the reasons for the delay in carrying out its terms: "I beg leave to respectfully inform you that, but for the pending litigation entitled 'United States of America vs. Jane L. Stanford, Executrix,' the estate could probably be distributed at an early day."

Mrs. Stanford cited this so that the legatees would be as fully informed as she, and further told them: "During my administration of the estate more than 200 claims were presented against it, approximating in the aggregate the sum of $1,600,000, and I take pleasure in informing you that all of these claims have been paid in full, with the exception of two or three unimportant claims the legality of which I have contested, but these would not interfere, in my judgment, with the final distribution of the estate were the case of the government against the estate finally decided in favor of the estate. You will therefore see that the estate is practically out of debt. . . . According to inventory values, the real estate in my hands as executrix is of the probable value of $869,139.82; and the stocks $11,843,336.00; and bonds $3,833,160.00, and it is from these items that I propose to settle the bequest in your favor under the will as soon as possible under existing circumstances."

In the fall of 1895 the Court of Appeals ruled against the government in the Stanford case and, in accord with the interest of President Cleveland and the Attorney General, the suit was carried promptly to the Supreme Court calendar.

In October Jane Stanford was again in Washington, concerned with the suit, and she wrote May Hopkins that Mrs. Grant and her daughter had taken her under their wing. The Ulysses S. Grants had been close friends of the Stanfords, and the two widows had continued that amicable relationship. Nevertheless, Jane's Washington stay was trying, and worry and poor health forced her to seek quieter surroundings. Characteristically, once away from the scene of her trials, she recovered quickly and wrote to her friend with refreshed spirit:

Great Barrington, Mass., December 7, 1895

Dear May:

I imagine your great surprise when you learn I am sojourning at Great Barrington at the Berkshire Inn. I have suffered very much from malaria and was quite ill all the time I was in Washington but excitement kept me from giving up. When I reached New York I consulted a doctor. He advised my getting to a keen, cold climate, and the same day a friend called and told me of the charms of this place where she had passed the summer. I packed my trunks and came on trial, and find it all and even more than pictured, for it is excellently well kept, the table much better than the large hotels in the city, for we have old-fashioned home cooking. It is located, as you know, directly opposite your dear old home. . . .

I have called to see Mrs. Cass and found her quite delicate, but up and about the lower part of her home. She is a most beautiful example of the stately, ideal old-time New England old lady of the old school. She was delighted to see me and could hardly let me go. I had to promise I would take a cup of tea with her tomorrow, Sunday evening. . . .

We had a very slight fall of snow two days ago. I feel disappointed it was not sufficient for a sleigh ride, which I had hoped for. I find the bracing cold air has been a great tonic, and I am enjoying Berkshire ham, jam, sausages, buckwheat cakes, sweet cider and wish I could stay here all winter for the rest, but my mind would not allow me for I am quite homesick to get back to duties which I am egotistical enough to think need me. I was advised by the doctor to go from here higher north by degrees as far as Montreal; it would complete the cure. I like that city and go after a few days at my old home, Albany, N.Y., returning to Washington in January. I expect, if all goes well with me, to be home the last of January. . . .

Dear May, one day I made a visit to the old burying ground where lie your dear ones' nearest kith and kin, and picked off some pine boughs filled with small burrs—I have them packed away for you. They sheltered the large tombstone with the names of the Kellog family on. I had heard Mrs. Hopkins tell of them often. It was a most beautiful winter's day, the sun shone brightly but not warm enough to melt the ice. . . .

Give the old-time affection to Tim, love for yourself and dear Lydia, and I thank you for your loving thoughts of Jennie. . . .

Always yours sincerely,
Jane L. Stanford

In February 1896, while the Supreme Court decision was nearing, Mr. Choate wrote to Mrs. Stanford about her will, which she had drawn herself. He pointed out that the aims she had in view were so far-reaching and momentous that nothing but the very best skill and learning would suffice in its preparation.

He further cautioned her: "One other thing you ought most carefully to consider. I am aware that your present purpose is to leave to the University substantially the bulk of your entire estate. But from some talk I have had with Mr. Wilson after you left, I think that it is quite possible that your estate may turn out to be much larger than you have estimated it. Now it may be more in amount than any university ought to hold or than it can be allowed by law to hold. Thirty or forty millions for instance might and probably would make the University an object of plunder and attack instead of being as it is now a popular institution. So you ought to consider whether you ought not to fix a maximum limit for your gift to the University."

He finished on a cheery note: "I hear nothing to change my belief that we shall get a favorable decision in March."

In her reply Mrs. Stanford, after assuring Mr. Choate that she was acting on his suggestion as to the preparation of her will, turned to the University endowment.

Kind Sir:

. . . I feel that it is my duty to enlighten you as to the largeness of my estate. If in settling up it reached one-third of the amount which Mr. Wilson has named to you, I shall feel very thankful. I have been going through the statements and accounts of my husband's estate since my return, as it has been necessary in the performance of duties, to inform myself as to the amount of the whole, and it is my brother's opinion, who is perfectly conversant with the affairs of the estate, and it is also my opinion that we are correct in this, our final, judgment as to the ultimate amount when the affairs are settled. I am very anxious, indeed, that all the residue shall go as I desire, and as you fully understand, without repeating it in this letter.

I thank you more deeply than I can express for your kind and tender interest in all that pertains to my welfare and the welfare of the University. I await with all the patience that I am able to summon the decision of the Supreme Court. I do not dare allow myself to feel that a victorious ending will come, neither do I permit myself to be despondent or fearful if a contrary decision comes.

I believe that an all-wise and loving Father rules in all things for each one's ultimate good, and this belief sustains and supports me.

Mr. Wilson has not yet returned to California. He is missing a good deal, for the sun has continued to shine each day since my return. Nature has put on its most beautiful spring costume and the earth seems radiant in its robes of beauty. All this he is missing. I am sitting in my home here in San Francisco with my windows open and this beautiful balmy climate has restored me to my usual health.

Please accept friendly greetings.

Your grateful friend,
Mrs. Leland Stanford

On March 2, 1896, the long-awaited telegram from Mr. Choate was delivered to Mrs. Stanford in San Francisco. Its total message: "My heartiest congratulations upon your complete victory."

The United States Supreme Court had rendered a unanimous decision in favor of the Stanford estate. Stanford had won its greatest victory. Of the Pacific railroad the decision read in part: "This enterprise was viewed as a national undertaking, for national purposes, and the public mind was directed to the ends in view rather than to the particular means of securing it. . . . The difficulties in the way of building it were great and by many intelligent persons considered insurmountable."

The record of what happened when the news reached Stanford is part fact, part legend, all joy. Some nameless herald waved the telegram and shouted the glad tidings as he raced across the Quad and beneath its colonnades. Doors burst open as students and teachers streamed out to join the victory parade. Up the Row they went; laughing, cheering, singing, dancing. A professor's wife said afterward: "I was doing the cleaning, and I heard all the noise and went out on the porch and somebody called to me that we'd won the suit. And do you know what I did? I sat down right there where I was and cried. I cried and cried and cried and couldn't stop. I knew Stanford was going on."

Back on the Quad Dr. Jordan was called on to speak: "Tonight you may do what you like, except to tear the buildings down or paint the professors." The amount of learning dispensed next day is not recorded, but it is known that the morning sun looked down and smiled to see yesterday's drab little post office resplendent in a brand new coat of brilliant red.

Now released from the caution she had insisted upon before the decision was final, Mrs. Stanford immediately sent a note to the students through Dr. Jordan: "I thank you one and all for your loyalty throughout the past year of doubt and uncertainty and now you can rejoice to your heart's content while I will quietly remain at home and be thankful."

The students invited her to come to the campus and share their celebration but she regretfully declined. "It will be best for me to go to some quiet place where I can rest my mind and enjoy the realization that the great incubus has been lifted from my life," she wrote to Charles E. Hodges, University architect, in acknowledging his congratulations. "When I feel strong and brave I shall turn my steps toward dear Palo Alto. I would be unable at present to meet the students. I am too emotional."

Two days after the decision President Jordan wrote to Mrs. Stanford, "Our celebrations are over and we have settled down to work again, a happy, loyal, and devoted community. And we all rejoice above all that the great strain is at last lifted from your shoulders and that you are free to do your husband's will and your own."

The correspondence files of the Stanford University Archives indicate that Mrs. Stanford answered all of the hundreds of congratulatory letters and telegrams. Many were handled by a short note, the draft of which is labeled in her hand, "General Letter," but many received personal replies. One of these was to Bishop, who had been the chef on the Stanfords' private rail car. "Dear Bishop:" she wrote, "Your testimony of loyalty and your expressions of interest are as dear to my heart as any that have come to me, and I have received scores from all parts of the land." To the financier John W. Mackay she expressed a thought that was paramount to her: "It is not the winning of the suit because of its advantages financially entirely that causes me to be grateful to God. It is the vindication of a name dearer to me than all else. I prize your friendship and thank you for your congratulations."

A note which she dispatched the day of the decision to Chief Justice Fuller of the Supreme Court was remarkable for its brevity. It said simply, "I know you are above being affected by gratitude but I cannot refrain from saying that I am profoundly thankful to the ministers of the law."

The favorable decision of the Supreme Court stirred deep emotions in Mrs. Stanford. In her special response to the congratulatory message from Mr. Choate she told of her amazement and indignation at a verbal message from C.F. Crocker, transmitted through her attorney, that the Southern Pacific Company was ready to share the expense of the litigation. She enclosed a copy of her response to Col. Crocker. Mrs. Stanford had apparently forgotten that from the beginning, in order to be free to make her own decisions, she had resolved to pay all expenses herself.

Palo Alto, March 16, 1896

Hon. Jos. H. Choate
Kind friend and counselor:

Had I followed the dictates of my heart, you would have been the first I should have written to, but the telegrams and the large number of letters which followed the decision of the judges of the Supreme Court added to the emotions which almost overpowered me when I received the news that the decision of the judges was favorable and unanimous. I was obliged to seek a retreat and went to San Jose, where I remained a number of days in order to regain my equanimity. I have been dictating answers to these letters every day since my return, but reserved this one to you until I came to this peaceful sacred home at Palo Alto.

It is needless for me to tell you of my varied emotions but I wish to confess to you first my gratitude to the all-wise, loving Father who heard my prayers and united Heaven and Earth to bring about justice to the name and fame of one dearer to me than all else on earth. I pled that He

76

would shed into men's hearts His light, wisdom, truth and the power which these possess to bring about justice. And secondly, I wish to thank you, one of the most prominent and powerful of His instruments used, and to you I feel profoundly grateful for your masterly efforts which helped to bring about the successful ending.

I have not been joyful or jubilant, for the fact remains that I am left alone here on earth with immense cares, heavy responsibilities, and perhaps vexatious questions to contend with in the settling of my husband's estate.

Although the suit terminated successfully, there yet remains with me the sad memory that my husband's associates gave me no support morally, no sympathy, and no promise of financial aid which the suit naturally would call for. I sought their helpfulness and their aid but they all positively declined, saying that if the case was decided adversely and brought against them they would conduct it at their own expense and not ask my assistance. Within the past few days I received the following verbal message from Col. C.F. Crocker through Russell J. Wilson, my attorney: "That the Southern Pacific railroad company was willing and ready to share with me the expenses which have accrued in the litigation necessary to conduct the suit which was brought by the government against my husband's estate." I was filled with amazement, astonishment, and indignation. The latter I suppressed and have today sent to Col. Crocker a letter of which I enclose you a copy that you will understand my reasons for declining their offer. My sense of honor would not permit me to accept pecuniary aid at this late day. The letter itself will tell you why, and I hope my action will meet with your approval.

If I am permitted to go on and discharge the duties which devolve upon me, I am anxious not only to meet with the approval of my Father in Heaven, but I wish to merit and be worthy of the approval of yourself and the many who have sent me letters of congratulation and sympathy. . . .

Yours gratefully,
Jane L. Stanford

Jane Stanford's letter to Col. C.F. Crocker:

Palo Alto, March 16, 1896

Dear Sir:

You cannot possibly measure my surprise and my astonishment when Russell J. Wilson, my attorney, delivered to me your verbal message which was as follows: "That the Southern Pacific railroad company was willing and ready to share with me the expenses which have accrued in the litigation necessary to conduct the suit which was brought by the government against my husband's estate."

When this suit was brought at the end of ten months from the time of his decease, it was so unexpected to me, so appalling and monstrous in its injustice that, even with my cup of sorrow running over, it alone was sufficient to crush my very heart out.

The suit, to a woman like myself, inexperienced in matters of law, not knowing at the time that it was merely a technicality of law and only a difference of opinion as to the interpretation of it betwixt the government and the railroad builders—I, in my ignorance, feared that the suit itself implied a wrong that would cast a cloud over the name and character of my husband that would be beyond our united efforts to remove. I realized to the fullest extent the difference it made bringing this suit against one who, when here on earth, had a power and an influence that was felt and far reaching, and who would have been able to defend himself. But alas, he had passed away and with him his influence, and he could not be protected save through his associates, who were as deeply implicated and interested as he, and to them I looked for sympathy, for aid, and for advice as to the manner in which this suit should be conducted. I assured my sick, sore heart that if your mother had been bereft of all that was dearest and best, a widow and childless, left here alone in my position, and my husband was appealed to for aid, he would have said the following:

"Give yourself no uneasiness. We will see that justice is done to the memory of one so dear to you and to us. We will take this burden upon ourselves and will, if possible, bring success. There has been no wrong done, we have lived up to the letter of the law, and we will defend his life-work and his memory."

In my confidence and trustfulness, in my great agony of mind, I sent Mr. Wilson and my brother across the continent and commissioned them both to see Mr. Huntington, the president of the railroad, and Messrs. Stillman and Hubbard, and to ask them what had to be done; if they, too, would be affected by a favorable or unfavorable decision in this suit, and would assist me by giving their moral support, their helpfulness, and sympathy.

Mr. Huntington's answer was: "I am not lying awake nights worrying about this suit. When it is brought against me I will defend it and pay my own expenses. I have no assistance to offer Mrs. Stanford."

My brother and Mr. Wilson then visited Mr. Stillman's room—Mr. Hubbard was not in—and Mr. Stillman rather ridiculed the suit and said he was not at all worried over it, and when asked if the railroad company would share the expenses of the suit, he most positively and emphatically said no.

I sent for you. I turned to you, my dear friend, . . . with your younger heart, which I trusted was still tender with memories of all my dear husband's affection and interest in you, which I know was great, and knew how ambitious he was to have you advanced in the railroad affairs, that in time you could come to the front and be its head. I remembered the sweet friendship of your mother, and I clung to you as a mother would have clung to a son, thinking I would have your moral support and sympathy in the great trial this suit was to me. You will remember I said to you, "Do you think the railroad company feels at all anxious concerning this suit, and are you anxious? Will I have to conduct this suit alone?" And your answer was that if the decision was adverse and the suit was brought against your estate, you would defend it alone, and at your own expense.

This at the time seemed more than I could bear. My soul almost refused to believe that men who claim to stand high in business circles could turn a cold shoulder to a lone, desolate, brokenhearted woman, the wife of the man who had been their president for thirty years, who had been connected with the railroad from its birth, stood by it through trials, tribulations, and persecutions. I was most profoundly impressed with the fact that I must not hereafter expect that which I had hoped for.

I resorted to the Father of Mercies, who has promised to care for the widow and the desolate. It seemed to me there was no one else to go to. I put on the armor of strength which came to me through prayer and determined to do the best that was within me to defend the name and fame of my husband, for these are dearer to me than all else in this life —and knew that I had to do it alone.

Twice I crossed this continent to see the highest officials in our land and plead with them to mete out justice or injustice speedily. I told them the facts, that I stood solitary and alone.

And now that God in His mercy has brought about justice, the pecuniary assistance which is offered me could not give to me that which I craved for, which was the moral support and sympathy and helpfulness which I had a right to expect.

I feel it is impossible for me to stoop to any material action that shall bring me down from the highest position on the throne of my nature.

Respectfully,

Jane L. Stanford

To this outpouring from Jane Stanford, C.F. Crocker replied:

San Francisco, March 18, 1896

Dear Mrs. Stanford:

I write this to say that your letter of March 17th has reached me and been carefully read.

A misunderstanding exists, which I regret with absolute sincerity, and will do anything to overcome.

Respectfully yours,

Chas. F. Crocker

General Hubbard's reaction upon receiving a copy of Mrs. Stanford's letter was one of exasperation.

New York, March 30, 1896

Dear Mrs. Stanford:

Your letter of the 25th enclosing copy of a letter of the 17th inst. addressed by yourself to Col. Crocker, came to hand today. My surprise on reading the enclosure was like that you described in its opening sentence. From the beginning of this government litigation I had entertained, and have frequently expressed, the opinion that all the involved interests would share its burdens. I have understood that an offer to do so had been declined by you and I think this appears in correspondence. The disagreeable experience of having bad motives attributed where good motives exist comes to everyone, no doubt: only my experiences of this kind have been multiplied in the recent years almost beyond the limits of endurance.

Very truly yours,

Thomas H. Hubbard

In this exchange of conflicting emotions, Joseph H. Choate stood squarely by Jane Stanford's side.

New York, March 25, 1896

Dear Mrs. Stanford:

I duly received your letter which enclosed a copy of the letter which you had written to Col. Crocker, and I entirely approve of the spirit of that communication. I think that the defense of the suit should have been assumed by your husband's associates according to their proportions, but, as they refused to do so hitherto, your spirited reply to their very tardy overtures is very natural and proper. I think they would not have made them if the result had been the other way, but would have left you to suffer alone.

I am glad to hear that you are recovering from the great strain of the last year, and hope most sincerely that you may now enjoy absolute serenity and peace of mind. You have certainly earned it.

The rejoicing at the University over the result must be great.

Yours truly,

Joseph H. Choate

Six months later, despite his earlier caustic note, Mrs. Stanford sent Mr. Hubbard, the president of the Pacific Improvement Company, the following cypher telegram:

SOME OF LEGATEES THREATEN IMMEDIATE SUITS AGAINST ME AND POSSIBLY ATTACHMENT. AM WITHOUT MONEY AND CANNOT REALIZE ON SECURITIES. I AM HELPLESS UNLESS P.I. CO. PAYS ME IMMEDIATELY THE MILLION AND A QUARTER DUE ME, WHICH I URGE YOU TO PAY. THERE ARE NEARLY TWENTY-FIVE LEGATEES REPRESENTED BY OVER TEN DIFFERENT ATTORNEYS HERE AND IN THE EAST, AND SOME MAY ATTEMPT ATTACHMENTS P.I. CO., TO MY GREAT DAMAGE AND THAT OF ASSOCIATES. MUST HAVE IMMEDIATE RELIEF. ANSWER QUICKLY.

MRS. LELAND STANFORD

Though her request was refused, the feared result proved unfounded.

Eventually Jane Stanford recognized her inability to understand and manage vast sums of money, and it was she who later effected a reconciliation with the opponent against whom she had so long tilted. Preparing to leave for an extended European stay in 1900, Mrs. Stanford paid a surprise visit to Huntington in New York. She offered her hand, saying: "Mr. Huntington, I have come to make my peace with you." Taking both her hands in his, he gently led her to a chair, then wiping his forehead exclaimed, "Well, I declare!" Jane Stanford added that it was time to cease harboring inimical thoughts. All tension ceased and they parted with a hearty handshake.

Both of these strong individuals had achieved their goals. Huntington retained the presidency of the Southern Pacific, from which Mrs. Stanford had tried to oust him, and under his management the company paid every penny of its debts, the only major railroad during that depression to avoid bankruptcy. Mrs. Stanford, in just as trying circumstances, managed her affairs with equal competence and kept Stanford University solvent and functioning.

Shortly after her arrival in Europe this letter was addressed to Mrs. Stanford in London by Charles H. Tweed, Southern Pacific counsel and later its chairman:

New York, August 29, 1900

My dear Mrs. Stanford:

I have received your letter of 19th inst., acknowledging the receipt of my telegram advising you of Mr. Huntington's death and I am very much obliged to you for the kind expressions contained in your letter.... It is most difficult to realize that he has really passed away, and that a life full of such earnest and strenuous activity has really terminated.

Mr. Huntington was very much touched by your thoughtfulness and kindness in coming to call upon him just before you sailed for Europe and spoke to me many times about it after your departure.

Yours truly,
Charles H. Tweed

From Bad Kissingen Mrs. Stanford wrote to May Hopkins, "Of course you have heard of Mr. C.P. Huntington's sudden death from heart failure. He never regained consciousness after being stricken. I cannot yet realize that this strong-willed man with so much under his control at last was controlled and wiped out of this life, as all mortals are, by death."

13

Dynamos and Water Casks

―――•――❖――•―――

$\mathcal{W}$HILE THE FAVORABLE decision of the Supreme Court brightened the outlook for the University, it did not at once lift the financial burden from Mrs. Stanford's shoulders. It did, however, free $2,500,000 in bonds which the Senator had designated for support of the University, the income from which was $10,000 monthly, far short of the amount needed to maintain the University. Much of Mrs. Stanford's own share of the estate, while potentially substantial, was not on a dividend-paying basis and required careful management.

In a letter to a friend of her late husband, who sought a position, she explained why she could not at that time increase the number of teachers or students and she made clear that selection of the faculty was solely President Jordan's province.

San Francisco, July 20, 1896

Mr. Alex Hogg
Kind friend:

I note all you say in reference to a position at Stanford University and hasten to let you know how impossible it is for me to recommend to Dr. Jordan in reference to any new appointments at the University.

I feel that the old friendship that you have always entertained for Mr. Stanford and the friendship that he ever felt for you warrant me in adding to the above that the University still is restricted and limited in its ambitions and its aims because of my inability to increase the number of students or the number of professors. The gift of $2,500,000 in bonds which I have by the grace of God been enabled to give to the Trustees for the present and future maintenance of the University brings in a monthly income of $10,000, while the actual expenses for the faculty, the President, and the necessary etceteras bring the sum total of expenses per month to $19,000. The $9,000 I am obliged to furnish myself through the strictest economy and husbanding of resources. Consequently I am not adding or increasing expenditures, but on the contrary shall retrench in the future.

My husband's estate is still in the probate court, and it may be some years before it will be released, as the legatees are still to be paid their $2,000,000. The above is another reason why I do not feel warranted in asking Dr. Jordan to add to or increase in any way the staff educators.

One plan that Mr. Stanford had resolved upon, and which I am earnestly endeavoring to follow, is the following:

That he would hold Dr. Jordan responsible for all the faculty and consequently depend upon Dr. Jordan to make his own appointments, and, if they were not satisfactory, Mr. Stanford always felt at liberty to make his comments and express his opinion as to their ability. And I endeavor as far as possible to carry out this same resolve.

Indeed, I am endeavoring to lessen my cares and my anxieties by casting all pertaining to the University upon Dr. Jordan's broad shoulders, who is far more able to endure and bear anxiety than I am.

At present Dr. Jordan is on his expedition to Bering Straits. I advised him by all means to accept this complimentary attention on the part of the government, as I was well aware that he was much worn and needed rest. He will not return before the middle or end of October next, and I will then present your letter to him, but I shall allow him to act independently, as I have always in the past.

Your sincere friend,
Jane L. Stanford

Though Mrs. Stanford did not ordinarily interfere in academic matters, she did on one occasion ask that an instructor in the workshop not be dismissed. Mr. Soule was one of three faculty members Mr. Stanford had recommended and who had been accepted by Dr. Jordan. The content of her letter to Dr. Jordan can be anticipated by her unusually formal salutation and closing.

San Francisco, April 1896

Kind Sir:

I meant to mention to you while at Palo Alto that I desire Mr. Soule shall be retained in the position he is in at the same salary. There are so few that Mr. Stanford placed in positions, and Mr. Soule was one; consequently it would hurt my feelings to have him dismissed. I remember Mr. Stanford making this remark in speaking of him—that he was not a scientific man, but that he was a good, plain, practical, commonsense man, who would teach the boys practical lessons in woodworking.

Sincerely yours,

Mrs. Leland Stanford

A year later Dr. Jordan had evidently forgotten Mrs. Stanford's request, but she had not. "I did not suppose," she wrote, "that it had ever been your intention to dismiss Mr. Soule. I always supposed you had received the impression from me that Mr. Soule was not to be dismissed from the workshops, but in our conversation I had gathered from you that you considered it necessary to have a younger man, one that is progressive in the workshop, but not at the expense of sending Mr. Soule away. I wish Mr. Soule retained from the fact that he is practical in every sense of the word, and this must never be lost sight of. He is earnest, always at his post with his work apron on, not so superior as to simply give orders and play the part of the gentleman and not the workman. Take care that no such man as I have described ever gets into that workshop."

Despite her intention of shifting the administrative burden to "Dr. Jordan's broad shoulders," Mrs. Stanford was constantly being importuned to handle a variety of minor problems. In the matter of a requested dynamo she personally inspected the power house to determine its need and solve the joint problem of the space occupied by the printing press. The latter would have to be removed soon, she concluded, to allow room for another dynamo which would be essential when the library and assembly hall were finished.

In a letter to Dr. Jordan she expressed her dislike for professors incurring debts, citing the case of a man who "has not shown honor or principle to find a means to marry and take a wedding trip east and thus add to his own expenses, instead of making an effort to reduce his obligations to those who have befriended him. . . . But the lessons are being learned by experience, and each such case as this present debt, and the debt assumed buying the library—which has by heroic efforts at last been paid—have had their effects, and sorrowful ones, on me, for debts have almost brought me to the verge of despair—not debts of my own contracting but of others that I am held responsible to pay."

The water supply on the campus was another petty problem brought directly to her. During a dry spell the only water available in the Quadrangle for over a thousand students and professors was kept in a wine barrel and tasted and smelled strongly of wine. The manager of the Stanford Bookstore called Mrs. Stanford's attention to the deplorable situation. "A young lady just came in to inquire if there is no place here where one can get a drink of water," he wrote. "On going to the barrel I found about four inches of very uninviting water in the bottom of the barrel, difficult of access and very unpalatable."

Dr. Jordan, the recipient of so many of Mrs. Stanford's directives, promptly received another: "I am surprised that such a state of affairs exists and no effort made to remedy it, for clean, good water should be kept in the casks. Will you kindly investigate it and oblige?"

But Jane's letters to Dr. Jordan were not always trivial or nagging. When he turned down the directorship of the Smithsonian she thanked him for his loyalty and praised him for the University's progress. She also showed her continuing interest in the women's suffrage movement.

San Francisco, October 23, 1896

Dear Dr. Jordan:

I read in the newspapers of the high compliment which had been paid you in tendering you the directorship of the Smithsonian Institution, and I also read with great thankfulness to God that you most emphatically expressed yourself as being ready and willing to serve the best interests of the Leland Stanford Junior University as long as you could be of use there. Now let me say that that blessed assurance comforts me more than I can express, and I offered a mental prayer of grateful thanks to the all-wise, loving Father that you had been led, through his instrumentality, to be the head and the front of the institution which was so dear to the heart of my husband and dearer still to me because of the great burdens which I have had to carry in order to insure its existence.

You have been more to me since my dear husband departed from

86

mortal life to the life immortal, in keeping at its helm, guiding and steering through the fog that obscured the sunlight. You have gained in strength and strengthened the University. You have gained in power throughout the whole length and breadth of our state and by this means added power to the University, and, thanks be to God, your power and your strength are of a high Christian character, which commands the respect of all the students and commands my tenderest love and gratitude. I hope and pray that as long as the dear Father keeps me here in the mortal life that you will stand firm and steadfast in your loyalty to the Stanford University.

I returned home day before yesterday and found my brother, Henry, in a very critical condition of health. I came back strong, mentally and physically, but since my return feel very anxious about my dear brother. Today he is better—more cheerful and appears stronger.

If all goes well I shall be at Palo Alto tomorrow, Saturday, and shall remain over Monday to hear Mrs. Chapman Catt speak. It has occurred to me that it would be very pleasing to Mrs. Catt to have some of the professors and their wives, if not all, sit on the platform with her. I have been asked to introduce her that afternoon, but this I cannot do—my natural timidity would not permit it—but I may sit on the platform if you and Mrs. Jordan are to be there.

Your grateful friend,
Mrs. Leland Stanford

A month later Mrs. Stanford again found occasion to praise Dr. Jordan for his stewardship of the University. He had just returned from his government-sponsored study of the fur seal of the Pribilof Islands and was on his way to Washington to make his report. She told him how he might ask influential friends in the capital to resolve her continuing financial difficulties with railroad officials.

San Francisco, November 24, 1896

Highly prized friend:

... It made me sincerely thankful to our good Father that in you I had so true and unselfish a helper and friend as your good letter indicates, that you should look ahead to a time when our sacred trust might need another head—God grant it may not come for twenty years. My prayer is ever that you may be spared to your loved, to the University, and to your humble friend to a time unlimited in years.

... I want to express myself rather freely on a subject I regret I did not mention before you left. It has been my policy to say as little about my financial affairs to the outside world as possible, but I feel sure I am doing myself and our blessed work injustice by allowing the impression among all classes to feel certain there is plenty of money at my command, the future is assured, the battle fought and won.

The railroad company has taken advantage of my reserve and silence, and the time has come when I will have to reach them through the influence of men high in position, men from whom they will have to ask favors. They hold the keys of the treasury and unlock it for their own use. I could ask righteous justice. I ask not for myself but that I may be able to discharge my duty and loyalty to the one who loved and trusted me, and loves me still. I am so poor my own self I cannot this year give to any charity—not even do I give this festive season to any of my family. I do not tell you this, kind friend, in a complaining way, for when people have pleasant surroundings, all they want to eat and wear, and added to this have those in their lives they can count on as friends, it would be sinful to complain. I repeat it only that you, my friend, may know. I ask of the company only justice to the dear one gone from Earth life and the living one left.

I am willing you should speak plainly to anyone who may question as to the University or myself. I have many devoted and true loyal friends in Washington, and I am sure, did they know I was kept from my rights, they would speak their sentiments openly, and, when it was known a public sentiment was in my favor and against their unfairness, it would cause a different course to be pursued towards me. I shall henceforth speak plainly, and I desire you to do so. You will meet our good President, Mr. Cleveland, my good and true friend, Secretary Carlisle, Mr. John Foster, and many others, and in your frank, earnest, truthful character can do our blessed work good and God will bless the act, and bring fruit to bear from the seeds sown. This is the only way these men can be reached. I have kept myself and my affairs in the background.

No one knows I write this letter. It has been an inspiration from the source from which all good comes—from my Father God. I trust Him to lead me all along the rest of the journey of life. He has led me thus far through the deep waters, and the day will come, for He never deserts the widow, the childless, the orphan. I have this promise, "Blessed are those who mourn, for they shall be comforted."

I write this to my dear friend, Mrs. Jordan, as well as yourself. You are one in thought and in life. . . .

Everything is going smoothly as far as I know at the University. The boys are wild over the game to be played. I hope they will win because my boys will be happy if they win. . . .

Your grateful and sincere friend,
Jane L. Stanford

Considering Mrs. Stanford's mode of living, as she herself has described it, the present-day reader of her letters and papers, as well as her contemporary public, might be justifiably skeptical of the reality of her frequent protestations of personal poverty and self-sacrifice. She was, of course, making comparisons with previous opulence. Nonetheless, following Senator Stanford's death, during the worst of a worldwide depression, she traveled by private railroad car with two servants. Throughout her most difficult years she was able to maintain her homes on the campus, in San Francisco, and in Sacramento and to travel extensively at home and abroad, always with a companion. For this, however, as well as in providing the needs of the University, she must be given full credit as a competent manager.

That her stringency was a relative matter was further indicated when she revealed that years earlier her husband had given her a substantial fortune in her own right, though it should be borne in mind that during the depression years which followed immediately after his death both her income and the value of her holdings were sharply reduced.

And it should also be borne in mind that she felt a responsibility for maintaining a certain standard as the widow of Leland Stanford and as the "Mother of a University."

14

"We of '95 appreciate your love."

———◆———

"*I* REGRET VERY MUCH that I feel unequal to being present at the commencement exercises. It is all too vivid—all that occurred a year ago when my dear husband and I were present on the same occasion," Mrs. Stanford telegraphed to President Jordan from Paso Robles in May 1894. "Please express to the students my undying interest in them."

Some time later from Washington, where she was preparing for the Supreme Court case in the matter of the Stanford estate, she responded to a joint message from the University. "To Dr. Jordan, the Professors, and Students of Leland Stanford University: . . . Your best hopes for strength and courage came to me when they are sorely needed and highly appreciated, as these delays exhaust one's courage and strength. Your loyalty and devotion in the past have been a great support to me and are still.'

Time revived her spirits and before long she was initiating plans for a reception at her San Francisco home for the graduating class and the professors, Trustees, and their wives. Her communication to Dr. Jordan intimated that party-crashers were already active in that day.

San Francisco, April 23, 1895

Dear Friend:

I have fixed on Saturday, the 25th day of May, as the day for the reception. I will let you know on my return the hours. I am obliged to see the railroad company first in regard to cars. I hope to be able to put on a special to bring the guests and return them to Palo Alto. I limit the invitations strictly to the graduating class, the professors and their wives, and the Trustees and their wives.

I shall be back in time to make the necessary preparations. I think it would be wise to issue cards to each of the class and also to the professors and their wives in order to protect ourselves, as in a city like San Francisco uninvited and unexpected persons might take advantage and intrude.

I leave tonight for New York. Miss Gertrude Stanford accompanies me.

Yours with friendly greetings,
Mrs. Leland Stanford

En route home she wrote to Dr. Jordan. Travelers of an earlier day will appreciate the difficulty she had in writing on a fast moving train. "I still desire to give a reception to the pioneer graduating class. I designate my city residence for the purpose. I also wish to extend the courtesy to all of the professors and their wives. Will you kindly give the invitations as I will not have time on my return to issue formal ones to them. I have arranged for a special train to take them and return them to the campus grounds. The day fixed upon is Saturday, May 25th, from 3:00 to 6:00 p.m. All Trustees and their wives will be invited. I would be pleased to have you and dear Mrs. Jordan receive with me. The car rolls so badly I can hardly write. We will soon reach Omaha and this must be mailed there."

The affair was a big success and long remembered. Dr. Jordan noted that most of the professors' wives had managed to get new bonnets for the occasion. However, other student matters soon drew Jane Stanford's attention.

New York, December 28, 1895

Dear friend:

. . . I must confess to a feeling of great pride in our entire body of

91

students, both male and female, and I think we are all in a way under obligations to them for their uniformly good conduct, and a desire to be, as my dear husband once expressed it, "ladies and gentlemen."

I note in the papers the discussion that has been going on between the students for the prize given by Mr. Lubin of Sacramento. I think it broad, manly, and deserves notice by the press. I wonder if these boys could not in the future take advantage of my dear husband's broad views and advocate his ideas in regard to the Land Loan Bill.

I borrow no trouble in reference to the University. We must expect such things as have occurred, namely the cheating at examinations. The exposure and prompt action on the part of the students in regard to the matter will have a helpful influence, and probably the act will never occur again.

I am quite homesick and have found it hard to beguile away the time necessary to remain here. At Montreal and Quebec it rained most of the time and the climate was unhealthy; therefore I hastened back to New York City, where I expect to meet Mr. Wilson on January 7th.

Hoping that this will find you and your loved ones all enjoying the blessing of health, I remain ever your well-wisher and sincere friend,
Jane L. Stanford

The "Land Loan Bill" mentioned by Mrs. Stanford was one that her husband had repeatedly introduced in the Senate. Its object was to make credit more easily obtainable by the average citizen and, though it never got out of committee, it has been said by some that it contained the germ of ideas that developed into our Federal Reserve System.

The youths who enrolled at Stanford University at its opening, shared its bright beginnings, and then all too soon the storm-tossed years that followed Senator Stanford's death were best able to portray the spirit those fateful times engendered. Jane Stanford's correspondence contains numerous letters from students telling of their gratitude for what the University did for them and their admiration for its founders. A member of the Pioneer Class expressed the general feeling.

Palo Alto, January 28, 1896

My dear Mrs. Stanford:

May I, as a Stanford student and a member of the class that was your favorite, take the liberty of writing these lines to you to express my admiration for your courage in this hour of uncertainty and my faith in our cause.

I can say with truth what you probably already know, that the University is with you, heart and soul, that we know and appreciate your noble self-sacrifice, and all that you have done in the past, and are doing now for us. We who reap the benefits of that self-sacrifice, who have for years partaken of the great advantages which it has made it possible for us to enjoy, feel for you more deeply than we can express.

And we of '95, who have seen the University at its birth, who have seen its noble founders watching over it with such loving care, whose future lives have been shaped by its influences, we of '95 watch with you for the first break of dawn that shall end the long night of watching, waiting, hoping, and fearing. This is my excuse for the liberty I take in writing thus to you, to tell you that now more than ever we are with you in spirit, and now more than ever do we appreciate all your love and self-sacrifice towards and for us.

Sincerely yours,
Charles Burnell, '95

The answer is not among Jane's letters in the Stanford University Archives, but as certainly as one can accept anything on faith, one was written. In response to a far less emotional missive, an invitation and two tickets for the first women's basketball game at the University, Mrs. Stanford wrote to the team manager, Esther W. Keefer:

Palo Alto, April 4, 1896

My dear young friend:

I received your communication dated March 2nd enclosing two tickets for the basketball game. Please accept my sincere thanks for the polite attention, which is satisfaction sufficient for me without the added enjoyment of the game. I have the usual weakness of human nature to highly appreciate all tender, kind attentions from the young. I sometimes feel that all I have left to me and all that I can claim in Earth life are the love and prayers of the students of the Stanford University.

Gratefully yours,
Mrs. Leland Stanford

Jane Stanford missed a good game. At the end of a lively contest, with many tumbles but no injuries, the score stood Stanford 2, California 1.

Encina Hall, the men's residence, which Leland Stanford planned with so much care, still stands. While Jane Stanford lived she maintained it in the spirit and purpose for which her husband designed it, and for half a century afterward it was a place where young men studied, dreamed, and played their legendary escapades. Newer dormitories eventually took its place and Encina now houses administrative offices; only its outer walls remain the same.

Mindful of her own and her husband's democratic beliefs, as expressed in the Founding Grant, Jane Stanford objected to having a fraternity in Encina because "it would make an exclusive set in the home which might be objectionable." Mrs. Stanford also objected to Jordan's proposal that a part of Encina Hall be turned into recitation rooms and chided him for giving in to the professors after he and she had discussed the matter.

San Francisco; April 3, 1897

Kind friend:

I have had a great prejudice against turning part of Encina Hall into recitation rooms, and I think, as the number of students has not increased this year but remains within the limit of 1,100, we should be able to get along until relief is afforded through additional buildings and not convert part of the "Memorial Hall," as I call it in honor of my dear husband, into noisy recitation rooms. My husband was always averse to using the building for any other than the purpose for which it was built, and I really feel Encina Hall would be very objectionable to live in if a portion of it was put to the use named.

My dear friend, I never like to be so decidedly opposed to any proposition that comes from you, for I wish to retain your support, your sympathy, and your warmest friendship.

I am convinced that this proposition has been made to you by the professors, and that it is not an original and voluntary wish of your own. You remember we talked this matter over coming from Sacramento. I could not consent to it without doing great injustice to my judgment and my sentiments.

Your friend,
Mrs. Leland Stanford

Jane Stanford heartily approved of the students' extracurricular events, but for each one—athletic, musical, or social—there was a proper time and place. She emphatically tells Dr. Jordan that Encina Hall is not for dancing.

San Francisco; April 23, 1897

Kind friend:

This morning I received the enclosed. I am very sorry indeed that they have applied to . . . use Encina Hall for their annual ball. I know the demoralization it would cause in that dining room and in the hall in general, and I also know full well Mr. Stanford's great objection to converting either of the halls into dancing halls. I remember well when Prof. Swain came during your absence and Mr. Stanford very positively said he did not believe in using either of the halls or Roble parlors for dancing. . . .

Your friend,
Jane L. Stanford

Mrs. Stanford enjoyed her work for the University and was grateful when a student remembered her. The following letter was in response to a greeting at Christmas time, 1898:

Palo Alto, December 27, 1898

Mr. R.R. Culver
Kind friend:

You, as "one of my boys," made me happier than you think for this festive season; that term lessened the distance betwixt us. It seemed to me another boy beside my own in the "Fair Beyond" had me in thought. I came down here to the University to escape the seeming loneliness that pervaded my house there. Here I felt I could find diversion in the activity going on in building the needed library and assembly hall, and when something came to me from two of the students, both calling themselves my boys, it touched my heartstrings. They little know, thought I, how deeply I am interested in their future life, whether or not they become noble Christian men influencing the community in which they live. . . .

My heart goes out to each and every young man within its walls, and after they have left I keep giving forth to them my strengthening prayers and thoughts. This is my work in life. God willed it so.

Ever your deeply
interested friend,
Jane L. Stanford

Whenever Mrs. Stanford returned from a prolonged absence, she was welcomed enthusiastically by the students. The following account is from the *San Francisco Examiner*:

Stanford University, October 17, 1901

One thousand students, accompanied by the University
Band and the Mandolin Club, marched four abreast to Mrs.

Stanford's residence tonight and accorded her a royal welcome back to the University after her year's stay in Europe. After the singing of college songs and a few musical selections from the band and mandolin clubs, Mrs. Stanford appeared and expressed her heartfelt gratitude for the welcome home which the students offered.

Mrs. Stanford told of the numerous costly and rare pieces of art which she had purchased in Europe to make the University Memorial Chapel the most beautiful in America.

The most striking feature of the evening was the spectacle of this great body of students passing the mausoleum where the bodies of Senator Stanford and Leland Stanford Jr. lie. Each student had his hat in hand and all joined in the University hymn, "Hail! Stanford, Hail!"

Jane Stanford's interest in and concern for the students, her "boys and girls," was heartfelt. Both as a group and individually they gave her many moments of unfeigned happiness. In a letter to Dr. Jordan from New York dated February 3, 1902, she chafed at unavoidable delay in returning home, but ended on a cheerful note:

... Before closing let me say a few words in regard to the dinner which I gave to the resident alumni. There were thirty-three boys present—two sent regrets on account of sickness and one on account of an engagement out of the city. It was a most delightful affair. The boys were in fine spirits. The table was beautifully arranged with American Beauty roses. I had very pretty menu cards of bright red with gilt lettering, and each one took away a souvenir photograph book containing all the buildings at the present time on the campus; these also had bright red covers and gilt lettering on the outside.

On the night of the dinner I was suffering with a very severe cold, and could not speak above a whisper, but the boys did the talking, and after the Italian band gave their musical program on their instruments and sang Italian songs, the boys helped themselves to the instruments and sang their college songs. It was the most delightful evening I have passed since I have been here. . . .

We thought of you, we talked of you, and we gave vent to our expressions of love, admiration, and respect. One and all sounded paeans of praise for the grand and noble work which you have undertaken and developed so faithfully.

15

Jewels for Sale

———◈———

BY THE SPRING of 1897 the country was emerging from its disastrous depression and Jane Stanford's own financial picture had brightened considerably. On June 1, about to take a three-months' rest and trip to England, she addressed the Board of Trustees, assigning to them certain personal properties to provide additional buildings for the University; specifically a chemistry laboratory, library, and a church in the Quadrangle. In accordance with the provisions of the Founding Grant, she desired to keep full control: "During my lifetime I wish to have the power and the pleasure of personally applying the property herein conveyed to the erection of said buildings." Should she be unable to complete them, she instructed the Trustees to do so.

Jane and her husband had often discussed the additional buildings they wished to see constructed on the campus, and now that funds were becoming available she was determined to carry out these plans. In addition to the three buildings mentioned in her message to the Trustees, she constructed between then and 1902 seven large Outer Quadrangle buildings, an engineering laboratory, and a mining laboratory. A second new library and a men's gymnasium, started in her lifetime, were nearly complete when they were destroyed by the 1906 earthquake. The huge sums funneled into these projects sharply limited any remedy for long-denied faculty salary increases or improvement in the academic program—much to Dr. Jordan's regret. He sometimes called this period Stanford's "stone age"—much to Mrs. Stanford's regret.

In her June 1 statement to the Trustees, Mrs. Stanford elaborated on the source of the money she was making available to the library, church, and chemistry building. "This property," she said, "which I give, assign, and make over to the University (which to me represents husband and son) is my own and has been mine since the year [1883]. It forms no part of my husband's estate nor of our community property. It originally represented $1,000,000 in bonds and stocks, but in the year 1893 I parted with 200 bonds of $1,000 each, which represented $200,000, for a purpose which I need not discuss here."

The certificates for Mrs. Stanford had been entrusted by Senator Stanford to her brother, Ariel Lathrop. With them was a letter from which she quoted to the Trustees the following extract:

To my dear wife:

Enclosed you will find certificates of bonds and stocks. These shares are very valuable. They are for you, and will secure you a competence in case of an accident to

Your devoted husband,
Leland Stanford

"After the year 1884," Mrs. Stanford continued, referring to the year of her son's death, "I felt it my duty to use all the interest for the benefit of God's children. This I did religiously, giving the interest to charities outside the University until the year 1893, when I found that I had to concentrate my energies and means upon the one trust so sacredly left in my care. The interest of this property since then has already helped to keep the University alive, carrying it through many difficulties."

In this first of five formal addresses to the Board of Trustees, Mrs. Stanford reemphasized certain provisions of the Founding Grant and issued some new ones, which were accepted by the Board as amendments to the University charter.

She desired that so far as possible faculty and students should reside on University grounds, and she called specific attention to the powers given the president which would "enable him to control the educational part of the University to such an extent that he may justly be held responsible for the good conduct and capacity of the professors and teachers." Experience had fully vindicated the wisdom of that clause and she wished it to be respected in the future, "both in word and in spirit."

Deeply concerned with the ethical and spiritual foundations of the University as well as its material needs, Mrs. Stanford concluded:

"I further direct that no ground shall ever be leased for a boarding house, school, or residence of any sort which shall be held for the benefit of any religious sect or denomination.

"I firmly believe all services offered to God are acceptable, for all contain the theory of religion. If, however, all creeds and sects would cast aside their forms of worship and all unite in thanking God with bowed head and bended knee for His humanity, that would be the life of religion and cause the angels to sing for joy. Humanity is God's representation of life beyond; God is all in all, and if we cannot appreciate and worship Him in all things we only worship part of God."

Though relieved of one heavy burden by the decision of the Supreme Court, Jane Stanford was still weighed down by the difficulties encountered in meeting the demands of some who had been named beneficiaries in her husband's will. Before going abroad, she wrote to her lawyer giving him in painstaking detail specific information and asking relevant questions on the basis of which he should draw up an informative paper for use by the probate judge, the Hon. J.V. Coffey. In substance her letter dealt with those legatees who had not signed an agreement approved by the majority.

She also asked that Dr. Jordan be consulted in her absence in all matters relating to the University: "I stand almost alone in this blessed work left to my care and I want and need his support and his helpfulness in this work as far as he can assist me. There are plenty who are interested in the affairs of the estate with me but few in the University."

The trip Jane Stanford planned was primarily for the purpose of selling her jewels in London, where she hoped they would fetch a good sum during the glamor and excitement attendant to Queen Victoria's Diamond Jubilee. Precious jewels for my lady's adornment and as symbols of the wealth and power of the giver have indulged the rich and bedazzled the poor of all races and climes since the days of the Pharaohs. Jane Stanford's gems were no exception. The question of their disposal had been raised two years earlier, but at that time she was too immersed in problems to think of going far away for any purpose. A telegram from the *San Francisco Examiner* in June 1895 read:

THE STATEMENT IS PUBLISHED HERE YOU ARE ABOUT TO
LEAVE FOR EUROPE; PAWNED YOUR JEWELS TO KEEP UNIVER-
SITY OPEN. WILL YOU TELEGRAPH EXAMINER AFFIRMATION
OR DENIAL OF STATEMENT AND OBLIGE.

To which she replied:

NOT A VESTIGE OF TRUTH IN THE STATEMENT. I REMAIN HERE
ALL SUMMER.

Jane disdained to answer the query about her jewels. They were private possessions fraught with happy memories. Never would she have
pawned them, but she already had sold several strings of pearls to help
defray University expenses when financial woe first struck her.

Before setting out on her journey to London in 1897, Jane Stanford
decided she wanted a souvenir of her husband's gifts and engaged a
painter to depict them on canvas. The story of this incident has been
told by Bertha Berner, Mrs. Stanford's secretary and confidante. The
gems were suitably displayed and she and Mrs. Stanford watched the
artist with anticipation. He seemed to be having difficulty in putting the
sparkle of the precious stones into their painted images. Thinking her
presence might be disconcerting, Mrs. Stanford left; whereupon the
artist drew a flask from his pocket and after a long contented swallow
turned to Miss Berner and exclaimed, "Now you watch me put a little
fire into that sapphire!" During the next several days, 'twixt the bottle
and the brush, he made the jewels glitter. Mrs. Stanford admired his
work, but regretted his weakness and was even more distressed when
she learned that a reputed copy of the picture of her jewels was on
display in a San Jose gambling saloon.

For once Jane's astuteness failed her. What with Europe's crowned
heads, Indian maharajahs, Oriental potentates, and Arab sheiks, London was ablaze with diamonds, sapphires, emeralds, and rubies of daz-
zling luster, and she might just as well have left her own precious packet
at home. At the moment there was no market for gems in London and
Jane Stanford carried her somewhat deflated treasure back with her as
she had brought it, in a handbag. Her jewels were destined for a brighter
future, one which she herself described in an address written shortly
before she died and which appears near the close of this work.

Though Jane's visit to Europe did not bring the hoped-for sale of her
jewels, it did provide a much needed rest and change from the vexatious problems she constantly faced at home. Wherever she might be,

Jane was a keen and sensitive observer. From the Hotel Metropole she wrote to Mrs. Timothy Hopkins:

London, July 8, 1897

My dear friend:

How your kind letter gladdened my heart. It means that at home I was not forgotten. The heart clings so to loved ones and more especially when our loved ones are among friends only.

I have felt more lonely here than I expected. The city is so teeming with humanity it almost overpowers one with its vastness, but amid it all I say to my soul, God loves each one and has remembered the hair on our heads and knows when a sparrow falls.

We had rather an unpleasant trip across the ocean—foggy, damp cold and a choppy sea with the exception of one day when the sun shone. We arrived in Jubilee times and London seemed utterly demoralized— hotels, streets, shops crowded with an excited teeming mass. The streets and crossings were dangerous, but the procession was impressive—gorgeous with gold-laced soldiers, magnificently dressed foreign ambassadors, princes, crowned heads—but above all else the interest was centered in the gracious Queen. She bore on her face all her goodness. I had a most exceptional opportunity to have *fifteen* minutes look at her. Her carriage had to draw, because of the street being lined with soldiers, close to the curb and under our window. The Princess of Wales sat directly in front of her. She is still very beautiful and young looking. The people went almost mad with joyous excitement and, while the Queen's carriage stood still before our doors, the soldiers, the crowds on the street and at the windows spontaneously sang "God Save the Queen." She was very visibly affected—one moment smiled and bowed, the next moment wept. She looked remarkably strong and well—her face fair and fewer signs of age than I expected. The story about her blindness is exaggerated very much.

London is scarcely in her normal condition—fetes of all kinds still going on, the shopkeepers are doing well, and all are cheerful and happy. The hotels are overrun with Episcopal clergy. They are holding a convention here in London; this hotel has a large share of them.

I like this hotel very much. My rooms overlook a little park which helps me very much to be satisfied for I can go to it, watch the pet crows, doves, birds all so gentle by being fed daily. This little green spot, so refreshing, makes me feel I have never been grateful enough for the blessed house I have at dear Palo Alto—its vastness, its varieties

101

of trees, shrubs, fruits, and flowers. I wish I had a basket of fruit from there before me now. I went out a few days ago to get some fruit and had to pay two shillings (50 cents) apiece for peaches and nothing extra at that price. California is an Eden with all its blessings. The poor have blessings unknown here. London is so filled with poor children on the streets, it makes one's heart ache all the time—they look hungry and eager-eyed for sympathy.

I never could be happy here—such great distance between the rich and poor, such abject devotion to royalty it amounts to servility—commoners are plebeians. It is almost as plain to be seen as in the time of the Caesars when there were three classes—patricians, plebeians, and slaves. Dear America is really "the land of the free and the brave." And may she always be so is my prayer.

You have made Mr. Nash happy for he loves to be with you. Give my love with a kiss to dear Lydia, the same for your dear self, and kindest thoughts to Tim.

Ever your grateful friend,
Mrs. Leland Stanford

Because of the excessive heat in London Mrs. Stanford went to the seaside city of Brighton, where it was also unusually warm. From the Norfolk Hotel she replied to a letter from Mrs. Hopkins.

Brighton, August 5, 1897

My dear May:

I was shattered by the sudden news of Col. Fred's passing away; it was so entirely unexpected that he had any disease. I saw him at my house only a few days before I left.* I remarked how marble white his complexion was but thought it natural. I believe myself that anxiety and worry had much to do with shortening his young life. I think you should feel thankful dear Tim is not harassed with the same yoke.

I like this place very much. This hotel is very quiet and refined. I have a fine room looking over the ocean and before my window each afternoon and evening a ventriloquist gives a performance to an immense crowd of nurse women and children. He has *five* dummy figures. All keep up a running dialogue, then all sing. He is really a gifted man to keep up such amusement without tiring the crowd. He is the lion of the place. I am surprised and pleased to see how easily the crowds here

---

* The presence of Col. Crocker in Jane Stanford's home indicates that their differences over the government suit had been reconciled.

are amused, and so orderly—no drinking, very merry, very kind to each other although strangers.

I may have to go from here this eve or tomorrow. I feel obliged to see Mr. C.P.H.* before he leaves for the U.S. I have not been able to get a stateroom that is centrally located for September 4th and, as I do not like to leave later in September, fearing the equinoctial storms, I have taken a central room on the *St. Paul* for October 4th.

I am glad I came here for I have been able to accomplish that which I could not have done at home.

With love always for your Tim and Lydia,

Jane L. Stanford

Mrs. Stanford moved on to Paris by way of Switzerland, where in a message from Dr. Jordan the worries she thought she had left behind caught up with her. She rebuked him for his action in a matter concerning some legatees, but was highly commendatory of his conduct in University affairs. She realized fully Dr. Jordan's indispensable role in the University, but while often lavish in her praise could also be sharply critical when she thought him wrong.

She wrote to him from the Hotel Meurice:

Paris, August 30, 1897

Kind friend:

Your cable message, "Home," gave me pleasure for now I shall not feel anxious about University affairs. I did not answer your former communications, knowing my answers would not reach you before your departure from California.

It was a most astonishing surprise to me that Mr. Wilson had overpowered your mind and influenced you to agree with him and asked *you* to inform me that my wisest course was to divide the only available income property at my command and not under the absolute control of the railroad—to give it to the legatees. If I had allowed it the two thousand five hundred given me by the Probate Judge each month which comes from Market St. property† would be stopped and the University lacking for its income. Not any of my wishes have been carried out during my absence, but a step I unhesitatingly deplored was an appeal to the Probate Court judge to have his honor decide and prejudge and give a decision as to whether or not I had the right to give land in lieu

---

* Presumably Collis P. Huntington.
† Presumably the Market Street Railway in San Francisco.

of money to the legatees who were dissenters and demanded extortionate interest from an embarrassed estate that had not the income to pay out.

I felt that you would sustain me under all and every circumstance because sustaining me sustained the blessed work under our care. Mr. Wilson used his very best endeavors to persuade me to give my personal property to the legatees and not to take the step I did in deeding it and my home in S.F. to the University. But my *soul* approved the course and I obeyed its dictates and did it and have never regretted it. I wish no more consultations and no further acts in my affairs until I reach home. It has been in a passive state for the past three months and can remain so until I return.

My health has been benefited by my three weeks in Switzerland. I return to London day after tomorrow . . . . I have made business engagements in N.Y. with the railroad company which may detain me two weeks, then I return home—where I now ought to be.

I had a dear, sweet letter from Mrs. Jordan last week. I hope you and she are strong and well and take up the cares and responsibilities with renewed love and energy. God will bless you for all you have been to me and the University. It stands out very prominent here on this side of the world.

I read an article in today's Paris paper—an address made by Professor Lathrop—favorably commenting on his advanced ideas in regard to the education of the young, and this subject reminds me to tell you I saw dear Mrs. Barnes* while in London. I am very thankful I met her; I know her better for I had a glimpse into her soul life. She has a sweet, patient spirit, hallowed by suffering. I am sorry, indeed, that a woman with her noble soul could not have been kept with us; we need such influence as she must exert among students and among all who come in contact with her. She will always hold a sacred place in my memory.

With a grateful heart for all your tender support in the past when the tempest of sorrow nearly overwhelmed me, let me assure you I lean on you for the future of the University far more than you realize. I wish the rest of my responsibilities gave me as little anxiety as does the internal working of the good work under your able management. I am only anxious to furnish you the funds to pay the needs required. I could live on bread and water to do this, *my part*, and would feel that God and my loved ones in the life beyond this smiled on the efforts made to secure the future of my dear husband's work to better humanity.

* Presumably Mary Sheldon Barnes, assistant professor of history at Stanford, 1892–97.

Excuse the blots and careless writing. I have poor ink, a poor place to write, and no blotting paper, but I found I had a leisure hour and felt it best to improve it writing a few letters home.

Ever your earnest and
sincere friend,
Jane L. Stanford

She was delayed in New York longer than she had planned and gave Dr. Jordan, also on a trip, the reason.

New York, October 25, 1897

Kind friend:

I shall be obliged to remain here for a few weeks and hope to see you before you return home. I am glad that all goes on well at the University. I always feel anxious when you are not there, for I remember so well when you were absent so long it lacked a balance wheel and I learned also no one there could fill your place.

I can advance, I think, the interests of my dear husband's estate by staying here among his associates. I have had a meeting with all of them and I have, I hope, made my situation as regards the dissenters well understood, and I am awaiting results. Mr. Crocker's death has complicated affairs to my serious disadvantage but I have not lost my faith in an all-wise, loving Father who knows all things.

I am much better in health now than when I left London. The summer's anxiety caused by the distressing letters and cablegrams from California regarding the action of the dissenters very seriously impaired my health. It amounted to refined cruelty. I consider my case badly managed.

Always your sincere and
grateful friend,
Mrs. Leland Stanford

To Judge J.V. Coffey of the Probate Court Mrs. Stanford sent a detailed account of the business affairs that caused her prolonged absence.

New York, November 15, 1897

Dear Sir:

It has occurred to me that I should state to you my reasons for so protracted and unexpected a stay in New York City.

You were kind enough to give me "permission to be absent during the months of June, July, and August 1897, and thereafter until further order of the Court."

While in London the most of my time was devoted to untangling and straightening out business affairs connected with the Vina estate. It had reference to large shipments of brandy to warehouses in Hamburg and Bremen that extended over a time of ten years, and nothing positive was known as to financial obligations on the part of the Vina estate. I was obliged to employ the well-known and established firm of Hollams Sons, Coward & Hawksley of Mincing Lane to help me solve the riddle. I found there were certain papers to be signed according to their judgment and this I remained to do, leaving for New York immediately after.

On my arrival here October 16th, my husband's railroad associates were desirous that I should remain in order to be present at certain meetings to take steps for new appointments and other business arrangements which have been brought about in consequence of the death of Col. C.F. Crocker. After various meetings some questions still remain unsettled.

After arriving here I received a copy of your opinion in regard to my course in reference to the six dissatisfied legatees. I read it with serious and heartfelt interest, and let me say to your Honor that I have ever, from the day that this sacred responsibility fell upon me, lived up to my soul's dictation of goodwill towards all without prejudice, without any self interest and with the belief that God and His angels were my helpers to aid me in doing what was best and right toward all.

I was driven by what most people would term persecution from those six legatees to assign them the property named, not because I considered the property of less value than their bequests would amount to in cash, but because I had no alternative but to give them an equivalent value in land, not being able to get from the railroad company the money asked for. I have reached a point in suffering and sorrow and care to be above prejudice, so it was not prejudice that actuated me to take this position.

There is but one piece of property belonging to my husband's estate which renders an income, and that is the Market Street Railway. It is valued at $1,000,000 and pays an income of $5,000 a month. Of this $5,000, one half, or $2,500, is given to me for "family allowance." The other $2,500 is regularly placed into the treasury of the estate and divided among the legatees. The $2,500 assigned to me I have been obliged to give to the University in order to keep it up to the standard it held during my husband's lifetime. Consequently I have not as yet had anything from my husband's estate to use for myself, but I have curtailed all expenses in the way of household affairs and personal indulgences.

I have given up all luxuries and confined myself to actual necessities.

I have endeavored to the very best of my ability to be patient, conservative, and considerate of the railroad company, knowing and appreciating full well that during the past four and a half years all railroads have suffered from the financial depression, more probably than any other corporations in our country. But in order to pursue this conservative course I have borne suspicions, unjust criticisms, and lack of sympathy which in some cases almost severed the natural ties of blood, and my struggle to be forbearing has almost wrecked my health and made life hardly worth living.

On my arrival here, in order to strengthen me with the railroad company in my endeavor to get more money to meet the claims of the legatees and also to give me advice as to my future course, I employed the Hon. Jos. H. Choate. I have had frequent conversations with him, and he, having carefully read your opinion, advised me to rest contented here and try to regain my health and peace of mind. From the fact that he interpreted your meaning as favorable to me—that the legatees should not be able to press me for money for a few months to come—and as the railroad company cannot furnish me at present the large sum of money required to pay these dissatisfied legatees in full, [I decided] that I had better remain here quietly until he (Mr. Choate) could more fully understand the situation and be able to give me a tangible course for future action. He is so sympathetic, so wise a counselor, and so good a friend, so well understanding all I have suffered and realizing my intense anxiety to be delivered from the thralldom of obligations to those whom my husband befriended, that I remained here the past month alone for this purpose. It is no pleasure to be on the fifth floor of the Fifth Avenue Hotel in a small bedroom opening on a court, economizing almost to meanness, when I have a sweet beautiful home to go to in the fairest of God's land—California—and which holds all that is most dear to me, but to facilitate and expedite business matters I have remained against my heart's desire to return.

I write this to you, dear Judge, that you may know I have not prolonged my absence in the pursuit of pleasure, but, on the contrary, I am attending strictly to the furtherance of business matters connected with the estate, and I consider it only courtesy due you to give this explanation.

Yours respectfully,
Mrs. Leland Stanford

Jane Stanford was in a constant struggle against forces which seemed bent on making her task of carrying out the will's provisions difficult, rather than easy and pleasant. Home again, she detailed her predicament to her lawyer and friend, Joseph Choate.

San Francisco, December 14, 1897

Dear Sir:

... There is no need for me to reiterate to you a truth which you well know—that I am oppressed to such an extent since my return that my life seems scarcely worth living. A few days ago I sent for Mr. Wilson as I had received intimations from my own nephew, Mr. Leland S. Lathrop, that unless I paid his legacy immediately a law suit would be brought against me, and yesterday Mr. Wilson informed me that Leland S. Lathrop's attorney was about to take steps to this effect. I remember very well that you said I need not worry about this special legatee because he had signed the agreement to wait until January 1st, 1899. Notwithstanding this advice I cannot but deplore that such action is about to be taken.

I have also had a letter from a nephew of Mr. Stanford, who is now in New York City, by the name of Philip Stanford, desiring more money. This letter I requested Mr. Wilson to forward to you that you might attend to this legatee, as he is in New York. He has been very considerate and kind to me and I really think that he has no resources whatever that afford him anything and he is solely and entirely dependent upon this bequest which my dear husband left him.

The other case which has presented itself is the creditor of a niece of my husband—although he has received considerable money on his indebtedness. I requested these two cases to be placed into your hands for you to attend to and I am free to confess that the legatees in the East, who are henceforth to depend upon you for consideration and advice, give me but very little anxiety compared with what I have to endure here. The demand for a little more money to be disbursed among them is just as painful to endure, and I do not know but more so, than if they made a larger demand, because it does seem to me that I should be getting a little something. There is no money whatever in the treasury of the estate at present. Everything has been disbursed up to date. Of course the sum is very small and does not go far. . . .

It appears to me that it would be very helpful to me if you could arrange with the railroad company to give me $150,000 every month beginning with January 1st, 1898, until January 1st, 1899, that would insure at the end of the year 1898 my freedom from the legatees. This sum could be disbursed as we thought best, paying off one by one or dividing equally among them all, and in that way pay the entire sum with interest due the legatees by the end of the year 1898.* Could you not get the railroad company to sign a paper promising to do this for me, and I could have a copy of that paper to show the various legatees what was going to be done, and it would give me release from this oppression and peace of mind as well. Can you not accomplish this, and no one else can accomplish it if you cannot, for Mr. Wilson is utterly ignored as well as my brother and myself, and upon your efforts in my behalf hangs all my hope. . . .

Since coming home, your assurance to aid and get me out of my troubles by January 1st, 1899, is more to me than you can realize, and my heart is full of gratitude to God that you are again standing by my side to protect me in my rights.

Yours respectfully,
Mrs. Leland Stanford

---

* Nothing came of this proposal.

16

The Estate Is Settled

*A*N OPPRESSIVE BURDEN was lifted from Mrs. Stanford's mind early in 1898 when she was able to finish paying all the debts and legacies under her husband's will, and the estate was released from probate. At almost the same time she began negotiations which ended in the sale of her Southern Pacific stocks.

In a letter to Mrs. Stanford, John W. Mackay, an official and director of the Southern Pacific Company, recalled that she had earlier expressed a desire to sell out her one-fourth interest in the company. At that time he had had such large contracts outstanding that he could not entertain the proposition. The situation had since changed, he wrote, and if she would now give him a list of her securities, together with her estimate of their value, he, together with some friends, would consider the matter. He added, "I may say to you that the market here in the Southern Pacific stocks is purely a 'made market' and should any considerable quantity of the stock be put upon the market it would have a very bad effect on the price of the stock." Mr. Mackay asked that his letter be considered confidential.

Mrs. Stanford replied that she planned to be in New York soon and would prefer to discuss the matter with him personally. However, when the time came, she felt unable to make the trip, but her interest in the possible sale of stock remained. She again addressed Mr. Mackay:

Palo Alto, March 3, 1898

Dear Sir:

Within a few hours of the time fixed upon for my departure last Tuesday, I found my physical condition would not warrant my enduring the extra fatigue without danger of serious illness. I have crossed the continent three times within two months and not allowed myself sufficient rest.

I regret it exceedingly because I was going on a pleasant mission in connection with the sacred duty expected of me as a loyal stewardess and a loyal wife. I also wanted the pleasure of paying large obligations to the seven legatees who reside in New York State and were not expecting to receive it until next year. I have now delegated the pleasure to my brother, who resides here; also to my attorney.

I have not given that deep consideration to your question which it requires because my mind has been absorbed in the matter referred to above.

I appreciate fully the value of the railroad properties at present and what it will be in the future, and how great an advantage it would be to the blessed work commenced by my husband in memory of our dear son if I let it remain as it is. I also realize we have passed safely through a financial crisis—debts are being paid, values are increasing—and, in paying out the seven millions which was due to legatees by my husband's will, I have striven earnestly to leave his one-quarter interest in the railroad untouched, and am glad to say it remains entire. I have also thought of my inability to manage business affairs of such vast extent.

I have been asked by another party the same question asked by yourself but did not give it much thought because I did not feel I had a right to do so until dismissed from the Probate Court and the estate be mine. This will now take place in a few weeks and I will then be willing to take into consideration your wishes if you will kindly make them known.

Mrs. Leland Stanford

For all her astuteness Jane occasionally erred in her judgment. One of her most serious mistakes was the premature sale of her Southern Pacific holdings to an international banking house. This was especially unfortunate because it was in the spring of 1898, when the disposal of

111

her stock was first seriously considered, that she had met a young Stanford graduate and lawyer, George E. Crothers. He was destined soon to become her close friend and mentor, and his good advice did much ultimately to place the University on a sound legal and financial footing. Regrettably, he had been unable to accompany her East as she had requested and where, possibly under a combination of unwarranted apprehensions and blandishments, she agreed to sell her Southern Pacific stock. She feared what the effect of another economic depression might be and also, at age 70 and subject to illness, she doubted her strength to manage such a large estate. Crothers believed he might have prevented her precipitate action had he been present. The $16,000,000 Jane received was turned over to Stanford University, but, based on later values, what Stanford lost by this early sale was $45,000,000, enough to have made it the world's richest university.

With the long and burdensome litigation over and the estate settled at last, Jane Stanford took prompt action against those who she felt had been disloyal to her husband's memory and to her. Several members of the University Board of Trustees were asked to resign; among them were the husband of one of her nieces and her husband's brother, Josiah. They had failed her standard of performance: "When my husband and I made our selection of Trustees of the Leland Stanford Junior University our choice fell upon men we considered staunch and loyal personal friends who, when the time came to act in our stead, would maintain the standing and dignity of the University and protect its rights by virtue of their loyalty to us in the past."

In administering the estate of her husband, Jane Stanford had kept two thoughts constantly in mind: "to maintain the University which he and I dedicated to the memory of our dear son, and to pay in full, as soon as possible, all the legacies which in the generosity of his heart he bequeathed to his relatives and mine." In both these trusts she had met with difficulties never dreamed of, and to those difficulties some of the legatees—not all, she was thankful to say—very largely contributed.

She had hoped for sympathy and encouragement from her niece and Josiah, but instead had been besieged by urgent and relentless appeals for money. "Had I been possessed of the money, how gladly I would have poured it forth to have saved the affection and love I had in my heart for both Agnes and Joie."

Edward Taylor, the husband of Agnes, refused to comply with the request for his resignation and protested his innocence of anything but the utmost consideration of Mrs. Stanford and the welfare of the University. Jane Stanford remained adamant and informed the Board that she declined to accept his services as a Trustee any longer. Josiah Stanford resigned with regret that he could no longer serve the University and that misapprehension of his acts and motives had changed Jane's feeling toward him.

And so ended another episode in Jane Stanford's five distress-filled years since her husband's death. She had made frequent trips East for estate and business reasons. She was now able to indulge in a short stay at one of her favorite mountain retreats, where her thoughts were of her friends. She wrote to Dr. Jordan:

Sissons, July 3, 1898

Dear friend:

I am here at Sissons Tavern and enjoying the quiet, the beautiful scenery, the fine moonlight nights more than I can express. I always loved the spot and so did my dear husband.

I went to Castle Crag first but remained only a week. I felt so hemmed in there. The noise, the crowds of people, the heat all combined to make it an undesirable resting place for me.

I am obliged to be home the 6th or 7th of July—hope to be able to get away again after a week's stay and will then go to Soda Springs where Mr. and Mrs. Hopkins are. I hope I shall find as much of God and His beauties there as I find here.

Give my kindest regards to dear Mrs. Jordan.

Yours most sincerely,
Jane L. Stanford

Her visit with the Timothy Hopkinses at Soda Springs proved to be equally rejuvenating. After returning home she wrote to May:

San Francisco, July 27, 1898

My dear May:

My trip home was all one could have wished. The drive from Soda Springs to the summit we will never forget. The grandeur of the mountain scenery, the luck Jennie had finding St. Joseph lilies, the amiability of our driver—all these features combined—added to this the setting sun, the fine cool atmosphere—all helped to make it a most memorable trip. Jennie was excited in her joy over the finding of the lilies. On reaching the summit hotel Dr. and Mrs. Jordan met us, which was unexpected and very pleasant. After dinner we sat on the stoop of the hotel and chatted until half past nine. Then Dr. and Mrs. Jordan (the latter carrying a lantern) escorted me to my car and bade me good-bye.

We hastened to rest and to my surprise I slept nearly all night.

My visit, dear May, will ever remain with me as a link with you and dear Tim, made stronger by having been brought in closer relations than has come to us since my dear one left me five years ago. You were ever dear to me, but your tender attentions while at Soda Springs were like those from a son and daughter, and it made me grateful and happy.

It was well I came home. An important dispatch had to be sent East and I await its answer this a.m. It may take me East immediately, but I hope I may not have to go now during the heated term. It is cold here and the fog envelops the City to such an extent I cannot see the *Call* building from my windows. . . .

God bless you all in your high mountain house—a home of peace and happiness.

Love to Lydia.

Ever yours most gratefully,
Mrs. Leland Stanford

A month later Mrs. Stanford was at the Vina Ranch. Again writing to May Hopkins, she told of her troubled thoughts and happenings.

Vina Ranch, August 29, 1898

My dear friend May:

My thoughts have turned to you so often I have concluded to write. It must have been a great shock to you when your young friend, Miss Adams, passed so suddenly from Earth life. . . . Had we known she was so soon to be called to Grace Paradise, how different we would have looked upon all she said and did. I would have asked her to deliver loving messages to my dear ones.

My thoughts have been running in this direction in regard to Russell J. Wilson. I am troubled sorely and deeply as to his condition, for he has interwoven himself into my life work, and I cannot reconcile my heart to all that would follow if he is helplessly stricken and unable to take up the threads of active life again. I have feared this very thing for the past three years. He is an active-brained man and should save himself from excesses of any kind. Our good Father has heard many prayers in Mr. Wilson's behalf from his loved ones, his friends, and the lonely and needy who seek his aid and know his worth and his loyalty —and he is full of pity and mercy—and he will be spared to us all. I cannot reconcile it to myself in any other way.

I came here last Wednesday to pacify a bitter feeling existing between white employees and Chinese. The manager had leased the grape picking to a Chinese firm, and white men had to go to them for employment and were paid and discharged by them. They rebelled and, thinking I had approved this course, they threatened to burn everything in sight. They commenced, and all the vineyard tools, ploughs, and so forth were destroyed—also 300 tons of hay and the same amount of alfalfa. I stemmed the storm, broke the contract, went among the pickers, spoke a few kind words to them, and in the course of a day all was changed. We now have 300 pickers, mostly white men. I dismissed the manager from this department, and I feel that it's safe now for me to go home. . . .

Good-bye, and peace such as God gives be with you all.

Yours always,
Jane L. Stanford

No sooner home than Jane Stanford was again immersed in University vexations. Though she and Dr. Jordan were in basic agreement on every aspect of the University's needs, they differed as to timing. Her immediate concern was to complete the required buildings, whereas his primary interest was in its faculty and students. Whenever an opportunity offered, the press magnified these differences into major policy conflicts, much to the annoyance of both parties. A particularly inflammatory newspaper article brought a distressful missive from Mrs. Jordan to which, despite her anxiety over the serious illness of her brother, Henry, Jane replied immediately:

San Francisco, March 25, 1899

My dear friend:

I snatch the first early hour of this beautiful morning and while my dear sick brother can better spare me from his bedside to write a few of my feelings called forth by the receipt last evening of your dear wifely letter. Not a word of it is objectionable to me and, dear friend, let me make a sincere and truthful confession to you. The very same feelings which caused the outflow of your feelings actuated me when I hastily left the sickbed of my brother, where I have almost lived night and day since last Saturday night after my return from dear Palo Alto, when to my great surprise I found him much worse and the doctor frankly told me he was in a very critical condition. All else, even my precious talk with your dear husband, vanished from my mind in face of the disaster which I felt I would soon have to face in parting with a brother who has been devoted and loving through all my life.

When the extract and the letter reached me from Dr. Jordan it recalled me from the thoughts a sickroom brings to one back to the other side of life. I read it hastily and hastily dictated an answer, and perhaps did not make myself clearly understood. The same spirit pervades me as regards the fame, the influence, the status of the dear president of the L.S. Jr. University as rules your devoted heart. I am as *jealous* and as hurt over an attack on his sayings as if he were my loving son. He has been the loyal, true friend through the past dark years of sorrow and anxiety. I almost forgot to treat him merely as a president of a university. I eased my heart by pouring out my woes—and he gave me glimpses into his interior heart life, and he has grown nearer and dearer. I regard him as the most truly truthful, honest man I ever met—singularly pure in thought and simple in taste, untouched and unspoiled by superficial conventionalities of life. And a beautiful characteristic—he is so just in his convictions and estimations of character. Even when obliged to condemn he praised the good qualities of the subject, as in the cases of dismissed professors.

I am astonished at my own ardent feelings when adverse criticism is made (which has seldom happened), when the press did censure. I felt it as I used to when my loved one was wrongly abused. I am as tenacious and eager as you, his best loved one, that he should ever be the foremost man in this Golden State—in intellect, in teaching the power of good, not only to the professors and students but his brother man throughout the length and breadth of this entire coast and beyond its compass to the far East. You and I know he has a powerful holding now, and I offer up prayers always that God, the all-powerful one, will guide, lead, and govern his ways, his intellect to the ultimate good of all who come within his influence.

I also admire the quality of independence of thought. I would think him weak to think always as I think, or as you think. Our views on expansion differ. That to me was a holy right of his own and I never for one instant would have thought I had any business to let this fact interfere with my high regard. My nature would turn with disgust upon myself could I be so narrow, so selfish, so contemptible. My obligations are a sacred part of my life, and, as I have to represent my dear husband, who has passed on to his higher life, I endeavor in a feeble womanly way to do all things just as I think he would have me. When I allowed myself to be interviewed and said what I did on expansion, it never occurred to me that a sensational article would meet my eyes in the morning—"Mrs. Stanford's views on expansion differ from Dr. Jordan's." It is not that we differ, as I have already said, but I felt sorry that it took an aspect of a campaign, and I feared political bitterness might be born that would rebound back against your good husband and my good friend.

I hope and pray ever that Dr. Jordan will be the ruling power of the University, the leader of intellectual leaders of men, the influence for good, for righteous living, tenderness. I love him as a fond mother loves a deserving son, and I love you for your true, noble womanhood. We are all closely united by sacred ties the world can never sever. The bow was tied by one passed on and has been tied closer by him since the loved entered into the holy presence of our Father in Heaven.

Let us then forget this episode; let us never think of it again. God, your Father and mine, reads our hearts and He knows all of us are true to each other. I need your love, your sustaining thoughts, your support and love. You have so many blessings you need not so much my love.

God bless you. I hope the dear doctor will not respond to my letter.

Ever yours most sincerely,
Jane L. Stanford

This afternoon my dear brother goes through an operation. It is the only safety for him. He is very feeble.

J.L.S.

On April 4, 1899, the *San Francisco Chronicle* reported that Mrs. Stanford's brother, Henry Clay Lathrop, had died of cirrhosis of the liver the previous day. He had been ill for eight years and had lived principally with Mrs. Stanford. Later she erected the monument, "Angel of Grief," near the Stanford Mausoleum in his memory.

17

Taking the Cure

———◄◉►———

WITH THE SURVIVAL of the University assured and its future in trusted hands, Jane Stanford prepared to take a longed-for rest and change. Dr. Jordan was notified of her plans, and on May 31, 1899, she addressed the "Gentlemen of the Board of Trustees of the Leland Stanford Junior University":

"I have invited you here today for the purpose of expressing to you my directions in regard to the future management and interest generally pertaining to the University.

"I am preparing to leave home for an absence of about four months, realizing fully that a much-needed rest and diversion of mind are necessary to enable me to continue my work in the future. Being of sound and disposing mind and memory, and mindful of the uncertainty of life, I deem it to be my sacred duty to so put my house in order that when I am called hence from mortal life, I can feel that I have done all that I could to further the great work which was so sacredly left to my care."

Mrs. Stanford thereupon stipulated a number of provisions dealing

118

with the Board and its functions—acceptance of gifts, budgetary provisions, and several other matters—and in conclusion said:

"There is another subject upon which I feel deeply, and I speak of it at present because this may be my last opportunity of meeting you face to face. Whereas the University was founded in memory of our dear son, Leland, and bears his name, I direct, under the power given me in the original Grant, that the number of women attending the University as students shall at no time ever exceed 500."

There can be no doubt but that Mrs. Stanford meant exactly what she said. Shortly after the Board meeting she wrote to Dr. Jordan:

"In answer to your letter regarding the number of female students to be admitted to the Stanford University in the future, I have but one thing to say. The number must not exceed 500 at any one time. I am not able to find your letter just at present, but I remember you mention that under certain conditions, if carried out, the number would be 550. To carry this idea out would be violating my instructions and very disappointing to me. I mean literally *never* in the future history of the Leland Stanford Junior University can the number of female students at any one time exceed 500."

But gradually increasing male enrollment eventually put undesirable pressure on "The Five Hundred," as the women students came to be known. In May 1933 the Trustees authorized an increase in the number of women students up to a point that would maintain substantially the same proportion between men and women as existed when Mrs. Stanford set the 500 limit. Changing times finally erased this resolution, too. In March 1973 the Santa Clara County Superior Court granted a petition filed by the Trustees permitting the admission of students without regard to sex.

The first letter in the Stanford University Archives from Mrs. Stanford's European trip is addressed to Dr. Jordan.

Bad Kissingen, Bavaria, July 12, 1899

Dear kind friend:

... I know you and dear Mrs. Jordan will be pleased to learn I have reached Bad Kissingen in Bavaria, where my dear husband and I have spent so many delightful weeks resting and recuperating. My heart cried out for another taste of this delightful air and the peace one finds here. I was thankful to leave London with its unceasing roar day and night. I was there twelve days. I spent four days at Windsor, one day at Eton College, two days at Oxford. Went through the dormitories, libraries,

119

dining rooms, kitchens, chapels, and could not but feel more satisfied than ever in the past with the accommodations furnished Stanford students, and if they could compare their luxuries with the primitive manner of living at Eton and Oxford—accepted so gracefully—our students would never again murmur. Tradition there makes up for all discomforts. I was amazed by it.

I expect to stay here about two weeks and then go to Wiesbaden for two weeks. I like this mountain air and enjoy the German brand of music. It distracts my mind and gives me pleasure, as it did when Mr. Stanford and I used to sit under the trees and listen to the music and build in thought the University. I am rich in sweet memories of the past which flow in upon me now that I am away from busy cares. I feel in my soul that God is good to me and rules in all things for each one's ultimate good.

God bless you and your loved ones and keep you from harm.

Sincerely, your friend,
Jane L. Stanford

Within a few days she wrote to Dr. Jordan again, following her practice of answering all letters received as promptly as possible.

Bad Kissingen, July 1899

Dear friend:

Your letter just received has given me so much pleasure. Most sincerely I thank you for the kind attention. I feel quite content about affairs generally at home. I came away with the intention to forget the drudgery, the anxiety, and care that have so imprisoned my heart and soul the past six years, and the good Father has assisted me in carrying out this intention. I am glad that my steps were directed to this health-restoring place in the mountains of Bavaria. . . .

The natives here and in the little villages around are a source of wonder to me. Their thrift, their frugal ways, their simple manner of living, and above all else their docility, their kindness of heart, and contentment are a never ceasing object lesson. Their little farms look from the mountain heights like so many patchwork quilts that our grandmothers took so much pride in making. The poor women here are the burden bearers. They bear the children, and the sons, as soon as they grow to manhood, are drafted into the Army. The mothers then help to till the land and care for the crops. Hard toil meets them each day and year, and I wonder how they can, as they pass the shrines that meet you along the roadside, kneel, pray, and be so happy, but I have come to the conclusion this very devotion and their religion furnish the secret of their happiness.

I am pleased that you are taking in a stock of health for the coming year. Human nature will wear out even if one is young and vigorous, and, as you never do things by halves but give the very best of your physical and mental gifts to the duties fallen upon you, you need to husband all you can, and not waste any.

After returning (if it is so ordained by our good Father) I mean to let affairs drift a little more without my personal supervision. I must if I want to keep well and strong. I am pleased to know dear Mrs. Jordan is with you in all your pleasures and that she, too, is stronger. It is hard to regain what one has lost. . . .

I expect to sail for America the 21st of October on the *Lucania*.

With sincere affection for dear Mrs. Jordan, and deep and sincere interest in yourself and in all that pertains to your health and happiness,
Jane L. Stanford

After two weeks' additional rest Mrs. Stanford wrote a chatty letter to Mrs. Timothy Hopkins describing the routine life at one of Europe's best known health resorts and closing with a dilemma she faced over one of her former Chinese house boys.

Bad Kissingen, July 26, 1899

My dear May:

I am very thankful to be able to admit I begin to feel like my old self before the tire and drudgery of business and care fell upon my shoulders. I came here to dear old Kissingen—so full of sacred memories because of my dear one having taken three cures here—knowing of its superior advantages for rest, mountain air, and its beneficial waters and diet cure. Not feeling well, I consulted with a physician and he voluntarily recommended this place and its cure for me. I came immediately, consulted with Mr. Stanford's good old doctor, Dr. Diruf, and, as he tells me he is "very content," I confess to the same feeling.

Two weeks ago today I began the strict cure, and this morning I walked and drank my four tumblers full of mineral waters, beginning at a quarter past six—feeling ravenous. My simple breakfast was *two* sticks of Kissingen bread, a very small piece of steak, and two small cups of coffee—no tea, no butter, no potatoes, no pastry or puddings or sweets or fresh fruits. When I reached here I weighed 165 pounds, and, even with the simple diet, gained 2½ pounds in one week because, as the doctor says, "It's all assimilated." Tomorrow I will weigh again and

121

I feel confident I have gained the same number of pounds again. In the evening, from five to seven, I drink two more glasses and walk one full hour—I can do it without trouble already.

There are at present—"the high season," as it is called—about 10,000 here for the cure—chiefly Russians, English, Germans, Poles, French, a few Americans. I was pleased to meet in the Kur Garten Miss Miller, and Saturday last I met her again with her married sister who, with her two children, had arrived the day before. The mother is with them; all are taking the cure. The sister is a fine looking woman, and quite attractive in dress and manner. They spoke of their love for you, and the one just arrived said Mrs. Caswell from San Francisco was on the same steamer, and in speaking to her about you as to how you were, Mrs. C. said "she never looked better and was by far, in her opinion, the handsomest woman in California." I tell you this, dear May, for it is a pleasure to tell good things.

I am enjoying every hour here, so restful, and I hungered for it and to get out of the prison house of anxiety and trouble I have been encased in ever since my "anchor" was taken out of my life. From here I go reluctantly. I feel at home in our old rooms at the same hotel, the same chambermaid so full of good heart for me, same manager, even the cup or glass fillers at the springs jump forward to get my water and hand it with a "good morning," for they remember dear Mr. Stanford and his goodness to them, and they know me as bearing his name. I could tell you many touching incidents that tell me how they here revere his memory.

I intend to visit Berlin, Dresden, Vienna, and then go to the Italian lakes for three weeks. I have sacred memories of the latter place, having been there three times in the past. I am enjoying it all with a very thankful soul for God's goodness in kindly leading and caring for me. In this good Father, who loves us all with a love which made Him give to us His only Son our blessed Savior—and there is no love greater than this —in Him alone can one find peace. My dear friend, Bishop Newman, has departed this life within the past month, and I truly believe he dwells now in the glory of Paradise, for he has drawn many souls heavenward that I know of myself.

Dear friend, before I finish I want to write to you about Kee. The Saturday before I left Menlo I met him on the country road between our gate and Mayfield. I was in my Victoria. I was surprised to find him looking so pale and thin. He took off his cap to me and halted as if to speak. I ordered Charley to stop the carriage, and Kee stepped to me—

122

and I said, Kee, are you sick? He hung his head down and did not answer, but I saw he had tears in his eyes and said, Kee, do you want to come back to me, is this the trouble with you? He said yes, and then I said I will see Mrs. Hopkins about it; I could not take you from her but when I get home again we will see if it can be arranged. I did not see you to mention it, but, dear May, you know I would not under any condition want you to give him up if you care to retain him. I have three faithful Chinese boys—Joe, Wong, and Charley—and, had I not been touched to the heart by Kee's devotion to me, I would not have been so indiscreet to say what I did. You are to keep him if you need him. He is faithful, trusting, and affectionate—I sent him away because he became quarrelsome.

I want you to deal frankly with me, dear friend, and I leave it to you to decide the matter, for, if you have become attached to him, I should have a sorrow that would not let my heart rest. I love you, dear May, and not anything I shall ever do will weaken the bond betwixt us. I have such contempt for anyone who will entice a servant away from anyone, let alone a dear friend.

Hoping your Tim and Lydia are well and having a happy summer, I am as always,

Your sincere friend,
Jane L. Stanford

During her stay at Kissingen Jane had an adventure in a fairy-tale setting which must have brought recollections of childhood visits with her father to the Albany Orphan Asylum. Driving in an open carriage through the picturesque countryside, she sought shelter from a sudden downpour in a nearby cloister. Outside, the building showed the ravages of centuries of weathering, its somber appearance accentuated by the storm. By contrast the interior, though furnished in utmost simplicity, radiated warmth and friendliness.

The Sisters conducted a school for the region's poor and were caring for thirty-four orphan girls, with others in day attendance. The nuns' habits showed evidence of much mending and the children's frocks were faded from countless washings. Mrs. Stanford was quite taken by the basic schooling the youngsters were getting and the preparation they received for the inevitable day when they would have to fend for themselves. On parting, she left a generous gift, but had an even more pleasant surprise in mind. Kissingen's dry goods store was depleted of its best black woolen serge for nuns' robes and bolts of navy blue cotton for children's smocks. The pastry shop was next raided and the accumulated bounty delivered by the coachman to the astonished but delighted Sisters.

A few days later Mrs. Stanford received an invitation for a return visit. A miniature theater with stage and curtain had been set up and she was regaled with a fun skit by the children, with many songs that brought laughter and tears to her eyes.

Before beginning this particular journey, Jane Stanford had bequeathed her Sacramento mansion, together with an endowment, to the local Catholic Diocese. It served as an orphanage until 1936 and then was operated by the Sisters of Social Service as a residence for dependent girls. Similarly her family home in Albany was redone and given to the directors of the Albany Orphan Asylum. Designated the "Lathrop Memorial," it was operated as a day nursery for half orphans whose mothers were obliged to work but who could take their children home at night. It continued thus until Mrs. Stanford's death, when the property was sold and the proceeds and endowment transferred to the parent institution.

Jane's thoughts and efforts had long been given to lightening the hardships and improving the education of underprivileged youth. In 1887, three years after Leland Jr.'s death, H.C. Nash, his former tutor and friend of the Stanfords, told about Jane Stanford's charitable works:

"Her grief, great as it is, has never interfered with her duty to herself, to her neighbor, or to her God. Her public benefactions are now almost historical. Her charities are widespread and include the support of schools, churches, hospitals, asylums, museums, etc. But especially have her efforts been directed towards educating and improving the children. Long ago she recognized the fact that in order to ameliorate the condition of the man or woman we must first improve that of the child and, acting upon this theory, she has pushed forward the great work of kindergarten schools."

Jane Stanford told of how she had become involved in the San Francisco kindergartens in an interview published in the *Cheyenne Sun* in February 1892. Responding to a young woman's appeal, she had supported a struggling kindergarten in one of the poorest sections of the city. Later she visited the school, taking along Leland Jr., then fourteen years old, and bringing candy, fruit, and toys. Mrs. Stanford confessed that she had been amazed at the misery and squalor she saw:

"I had lived all my life up to that time entirely for my own pleasures, but the experience of that day and the joy expressed by those little children over the insignificant gifts that I had brought them opened my eyes to a phase of life that I did not realize existed, and I thank God I have never closed them since. . . . When we came out my boy said, 'Mamma, I think that is the best thing you ever did in your life.' . . . My whole life changed from that hour: my manner and thought changed, my very soul was created anew. But I can never live down those wasted years. . . ."

Mrs. Stanford established and maintained six free kindergartens in San Francisco where over 500 children of both sexes, between the ages of two and seven, received their first instruction. In addition, she supported a free kindergarten in Menlo Park and one at Mayfield—the towns on either side of the Stanford campus—each with more than thirty children in attendance. At the Palo Alto Farm she provided higher grade instruction by two competent teachers for the men and boys employed there. Her love of music, so evident in her interest in the choir of Stanford Memorial Church, caused her to provide a free singing class under a professor of music at Menlo Park. It was attended by some forty students who provided much pleasure for themselves and the community.

18

Sandstone or Professors?

No DOUBT INFLUENCED by her removal from the immediacy of University affairs, Jane Stanford's thoughts turned ever more toward the high hopes she had for its spiritual and moral values. From the Swiss Alps she wrote to Dr. Jordan:

Rigi-Scheidegg, Switzerland, September 5, 1899

Kind friend:

Naturally my mind has been dwelling a good deal upon the internal workings of the University. I have such hopes and ambitions for its future as I have never dared to express, for the one capital theme of my thoughts hitherto has been the financial problem.

I have resolved to keep the University on the highest level morally and spiritually. The latter is more deeply interesting to me from the fact that it seems to be lost sight of in a sense. Last Sunday, here on the top of this grand mountain, I heard one of the best sermons that I have listened to since I have been in Europe, preached by an English clergy-

man and, among very many good things which he said, he made a remark that science was very well in its place, education was a necessity,
but all this was like tingling sounding brass without the development of
the soul, without heeding the doctrines preached by our Savior, and
without fitting oneself for the life that is to follow this.

I think that Ingersoll* was a living example of this truth. Morally he
was a good man, he obeyed the laws of his country, he was affectionate
and devoted to his family and to his friends. God gave him brilliant
talents and he made use of them to tear down the support of many a
man and woman on earth, and could give them nothing in place to lean
upon. He died without ever having acknowledged his God, his Savior,
or the life beyond. What monument has he left behind? What consolation has his family? And worse than all else, what must have been his
thoughts and his feelings as he awoke? If he could only be allowed to
come back and speak to his loved ones and say to them, have faith in
God and in the rewards of a well-spent life. Ingersoll's life and Ingersoll's
death were not much above the life and death of an animal.

I am thinking very seriously on the subject because I am deeply interested in establishing a chair of Christian Philosophy or Ethics, or whatever you may term it, for developing the soul-life of the students, if it is
possible to be done. . . . I speak of this now as my health has improved
so much, I feel it is going to be a great pleasure to me to take a more active interest in the internal workings of the University than I ever have
before.

I have just written socially to dear Mrs. Jordan; consequently my letter to you lacks a social side.

Sincerely, your friend,
Jane L. Stanford

Back home, her mind was again focused upon the University's material needs. In apparent contradiction to her previous letter, she wrote to
Dr. Jordan that she could not consider faculty expansion at this time.

San Francisco; December 16, 1899

Kind friend:

Your letter dated December 9th has been received and considered.
Very briefly I wish to express myself in regard to further expansion at
the present time. My aim and my prayers have been in the past, and are
still, to put up the buildings that face the Inner Quadrangle already being used, and I feel an intense sense of thankfulness that I have been

---

* Robert Green Ingersoll, lawyer, politician, and noted agnostic lecturer.

permitted to do this much. These buildings and the chemical building are all that I can possibly consent to this coming year.

I have thought much on these lines, feeling sure I would be pleasing the dear one gone to go on slowly and not expend money for an additional number of students, professors, or teachers. Fourteen hundred students for the next few years are sufficient for us to care for. The running expenses must be kept where they are until I feel thoroughly justified in further expanding and enlarging.

I note what you have written in regard to the Engineering Department. A young institution cannot expect in its infancy to be equipped on an equality with Cornell or the Massachusetts Institute of Technology in special departments. There are in the East you say, twenty colleges with better engineering equipment than we have. They probably are older by many years and supported by a generous public and students themselves aiding. Marine engineering and architecture no doubt will come in the future, as also the arts.

I would greatly appreciate taking a little ease after my hard struggle and many personal deprivations of six years and a half, and I cannot but feel in a sense appalled at the big sums you quote. Even with the blessing that has come to me, it would be inadequate to meet the demands if the University is now increased along the lines proposed. Let me say even at the cost of repeating myself, I intend to keep just where we are at present as far as the payroll and other expenditures of money are concerned.

Yours respectfully,
Jane L. Stanford

During the opening months of the new century Mrs. Stanford was busy putting her personal affairs in order preliminary to making another extended trip abroad. Between exchanges with the officers of the Southern Pacific Company and the Pacific Improvement Company, she showed concern for the man who had been Leland Jr.'s tutor, then Mr. Stanford's and her secretary, and lastly the University librarian. On April 28, 1900, she wrote to President Jordan:

"Would it be possible for you to allow Mr. Nash to be released from his duties immediately. I find him quite ill, and if he does not care for himself now he may be a sufferer for some time to come. A vacation now will restore him soon. I have insisted on his having a physician and will see that he has close attention. The rest is in your power to do. Of course he will remonstrate against the release—I know him so well—but it is an absolute necessity. He would disapprove of my asking this of you; he really does not realize his condition. The end of the term is so near it cannot fall hard on the others in the library to fill his duties."

Also, Jane did not forget her boys and girls:

"Mrs. Stanford extends an invitation to the students of Stanford University to attend a reception to be given to them at her home at Palo Alto on Tuesday, May the first, nineteen hundred, from three to six o'clock, p.m."

Her next several letters are from Bad Kissingen and Paris. They are replete with personal experiences, broad impressions, and thoughts about the University.

Bad Kissingen, August 9, 1900

Dr. David Starr Jordan
Highly prized friend:

Imagine my surprise this morning, on sitting down to breakfast and taking up my daily Paris *New York Herald*, to find this headline: "China cannot be conquered, Dr. David Starr Jordan writes to the *New York Herald* from the Far East." Of course, breakfast was suspended until I had read the article through. As it was merely a synopsis of your letter to the *Herald*, I am now very anxious to see the entire letter, but from what I have gleaned from this short article I am satisfied that you have diagnosed the situation openly, clearly, and satisfactorily.

So few dare to tell the truth in regard to these foreign missionaries in China. Mr. Stanford and I, in years past and gone, had no sympathy whatever with these missionaries, who were so anxious to leave home —many of them because of poor surroundings and want of comforts of life, and as a relief sought a home among the heathens, where they were well provided for, had comfortable homes and natives at the command of every member of the family to do the hard work, and, in many instances, these natives receiving no compensation whatever. Selfishness has been the keynote among the majority of the foreign missionaries. I do make an exception of the Roman Catholic priests and sisters, for they make sacrifices right here at home, and the same in foreign countries.

Of course you must expect that the Christian churches will each come to the rescue of their missionaries abroad and try to counteract your letter, but it is full of truths and will meet the approbation and the approval of the good common-sensed men and women independent of churches throughout our whole land.

You were kind enough to write me on the steamer *Gaelic* off the coast of Japan. Your letter was more than ordinarily welcome. I was glad to know that you were well and having a pleasant trip. I also received a letter from dear Mrs. Jordan and was pleased to hear that she and the children were not only well but having a delightful time. Her surroundings seemed to be to her entire satisfaction, and she was not being bored with being obliged to act as hostess which, of course, must be a great relief to her.

I find the charm of being here is the fact that I am never in fear of being invaded at an unwelcome hour. I am resting in every sense of the word. I have been here now eleven days, took one week to recover from the intense heat of London and Paris, which confined me to my room. I made no effort to go out at all, saw nothing of the Exposition, and had no desire to. I commenced the cure four days ago and, according to the doctor's advice, will drink the waters for four weeks. . . .

I take special note of what you have said to me regarding the conservatory of music in connection with the Stanford University. As yet I have not mentioned the subject to Mr. Stanford.* As time passes and circumstances develop, I may feel emboldened to make known to him what would give me pleasure in this respect. I have been so tenderly and mercifully guided by the all-wise heavenly Father that I dare not say I wish this or I wish that from any outsider, even Mr. Stanford's brother. My heart is so filled with gratitude that I am permitted to do what I am doing that I sometimes feel it may be an evidence of selfishness to wish for outside help in any department when I have been blessed to be able to carry out the wishes of my dear husband.

My health is fairly good. I expect the rest, the strict diet, and constant exercise which I am now pursuing will be of great benefit to me the coming year, and whatever I wish for myself, dear friend, I wish the same for you, that you may be sustained physically and mentally, strengthened by wisdom that comes from on high, and that the University under your fostering care may be blessed way beyond your expectations. . . .

Most truly,
Mrs. Leland Stanford

As the days passed, Jane's thoughts turned toward Stanford and home.

Bad Kissingen, August 31, 1900

Dear Mrs. Jordan:

As the month of September draws near my thoughts dwell more and

* Presumably Thomas Welton Stanford.

130

more on dear Palo Alto. I picture the busy scene there—students returning, retinue of carriages rushing up the main drive up to the Arch—and
I can see the artists at work on the carving, bringing out the story of
civilization of the world and prevailing my entire being. Such a sense
of gratitude fills my soul that I, so unworthy of God's special care,
should have been chosen as an humble instrument to do the will of the
loved ones gone on to their reward for lives well spent.

About this time you, my dear friend, are anxiously looking for the one
whom you hold dearest and best of all earthly loves. I join you in your
prayers that he may return safe and well. I feel so content when the
supreme head is at his post guiding the great institution that is being
moulded and fashioned by his liberal and advanced ideas as to what is
best for the men and women for their future lives, and those with whom
they come in contact. I am so desirous to have the souls of our students
enlightened, developed, and that they be made to feel they have souls
worthy of notice and cultivation. I always remember how this soul development came late in life to my dear husband and my poor self, but
it changed the whole world to us both. And I do so want the dear boys
to be men of honor and high aims, and the dear girls women of superior
quality that will make them grand wives and tender Christian mothers.
What is worse to contemplate than a Godless man, and worse still a
Godless woman?

Now let me tell you about myself. I have been here nearly four weeks
—have let up on the cure for one week, as the doctor thought it advisable, and took advantage of this opportunity to go to the Passion Play
at Oberammergau—was there on the 25th of August, my seventy-sec-
ond birthday. I was there ten years ago last July. Mr. Stanford was here
for the cure, and my brother, Henry, who was here with us, attended
me to the play. It was better given this year and there are more comforts
to be found at Oberammergau. I stayed as I did ten years ago with a
native Bavarian family and enjoyed that feature.

After the 25th I took a carriage and visited the two famous castles of
Ludwig Second. Had a charming drive of eight hours through the Bavarian and Austrian Alps. The beauty of it is beyond description—the
castles seemed tawdry and barbaric in splendor but sunk into insignif-
icance compared to the works of God outside of the castle windows.
En route there I went to Munich and staid half a day and night at Nu-
remberg. I returned in time to commence two weeks more of cure and
leave here the 15th of September. Will go for two weeks after the cure
in the Austrian Alps, winding up, God willing, at Paris October 3rd.

I am feeling so quieted in mind and body since I came here. I love this quiet, quaint Bavarian village. The people are so simple, honest, trusting. . . .

I have just had a call from a friend who tells me she has had a letter dated from London from Mrs. T. Hopkins. She goes to Carlsbad for a cure and returns to California in October. I shall try and see her there.

I hope this will find you back home, your dear self and your children well and strong—and the dear Doctor united with you all.

Ever yours most sincerely,
Mrs. Leland Stanford

Just before leaving Bad Kissingen, Jane heard from May Hopkins and was delighted to learn that she had been helped by the waters at Carlsbad. Jane cautioned her friend not to take the waters too heroically and to live up to the diet rules. She was able to tell May that, with one exception, she, too, had benefited. The pangs of hunger were not among the tribulations that Jane Stanford had ever been called upon to bear, and her weight apparently had become uncontrollable. "I have lived up strictly to old Dr. Diruf's orders and am now able to walk five miles a day with ease and, if conditions are favorable, walk seven. I am dieting strictly but have gained four pounds. I leave for Paris tomorrow morning, stay overnight at Frankfort, the next day go to Metz and stay two days and nights. Jennie has been there one month at a branch of the Paris Sacred Heart Convent. She has a special Sister to care for her, teach her French so that she can enter the Sacred Heart of Paris October 3rd and go into a class of her own age. She enters there for one year, giving special attention to French, German, and music—also history. They do not allow a word spoken but French. Jennie thought she knew French at home but it did not amount to anything. I am eager to see her —I hear from her twice a week. I will take her by surprise. . . ."

From the Hotel Meurice, Paris, Jane gave May the sad news of Barbara Jordan's death.

Paris, September 23, 1900

Dearest May:

Your kind letter dated September 21st I found on my table on my return a few moments since from church. . . .

I shall be brief as the time for writing happens to be limited—as I have an engagement. I write now and not later because I am anxious to tell you of the sad news that came to me by cablegram from my brother, Charles, telling of the death of Barbara Jordan on the 15th of September. The Doctor had not yet arrived from his trip to Japan, but was expected the next day. What a distressing homecoming for him, and how pitiful for both parents that at such a time they were so widely separated. Dear Mrs. Jordan has had her mother heart tried beyond all other trials that ever before have come to her. The dear Doctor idolized this precious gift from God. I can only pray for them that our good Father, who gave them their children, will in His own way shed light, peace, and resignation to His will.

I remain here till the 14th of October and then, if I continue well, I start for Italy, staying a few weeks at the largest cities, going as far as Sorrento, stopping a few days at Castellammare, where I passed a week with my dear son in 1880. I will take a steamer from Naples to go to Alexandria en route to Egypt.

I have made two visits to the Exposition. I take it in small doses—there is much that is chaff that one can see in all fairs. The picture gallery has a portrait of Queen Victoria that excels all else in the great collection. I hope you will try and see it. Give my kind regards to Mrs. and Miss Kohl. To Tim and Lydia my tender love. For yourself, dear May, the same love that I have felt for you.

Yours faithfully,
Mrs. Leland Stanford

In spite of personal sorrow, the wants of the University continued to receive the full attention of Dr. Jordan and Mrs. Stanford. She agreed to do what she could to provide the needed books he had requested but cautioned him: "Of course you know, dear friend, that whatever I have to spend must be spent carefully and judiciously, as there is not enough of income to give all the necessary needs, while the necessary and most important buildings are being erected." She respected Dr. Jordan's wishes, for she knew he held at heart the future of the University almost as sacredly and closely as she did. But she was not so sure of some others: "The professors as a rule (but there are exceptions, and golden exceptions) think they want many things that they can do without. It is so easy to spend money, but, oh, how hard it is to get it you and I know."

A few weeks later she cabled him that he could buy a much desired set of "Parliamentary Papers 1805–1879" for $1,500, but ended a short note with "P.S. I will not feel justified in spending any more for books this year. J.L.S."

19

Academic Freedom on Trial

DURING THE REST of her hoped for pleasure trip Jane Stanford was too preoccupied with affairs at home to enjoy fully the scenes about her. In order to appreciate the reason for this, the chronology of her journey must be interrupted with two communications of an earlier date. The first rumbling of a conflict which was to nearly tear the University apart was heard in this blunt message from Mrs. Stanford to its President:

San Francisco, January 18, 1897

Dear Dr. Jordan:

I send you a clipping which was sent to me, without comment.

The fact that Prof. Ross would speak before a gathering of Socialists was sufficient to warrant me to say all I did to you in regard to his being retained at the University.

Yours respectfully,
Mrs. Leland Stanford

This is not the time or place to retry a case, long since closed, involving the issue of academic freedom; but enough must be said about the "Ross Affair," as it came to be known in Stanford annals, to grasp something of its emotional impact on Jane Stanford, President Jordan, the campus community, and indeed, the whole scholastic world.

Edward A. Ross, professor of economic theory and finance, was young, gifted, articulate. Arriving two years after the University opened, he was warmly received by faculty and students, and a brilliant future for him at Stanford seemed assured. It was not long, however, before less desirable traits began to surface: dogmatic assertiveness on debatable issues, a gift for the caustic phrase, and an unscholarly predilection for the press interview.

Such manifestations were passed over by Dr. Jordan as youthful ebullition which further experience and the example of wiser heads would overcome. Not so. The divisive social issues of the McKinley-Bryan presidential campaign of 1896, "free silver" versus "sound money," were properly debated on the campus. Dr. Ross, however, brought the University name into newspaper headlines and public discussion with inflammatory speeches off-campus and partisan tracts.

In a letter to Dr. Jordan Mrs. Stanford gave her views on the broad question of personal freedom with clarity and force.

San Francisco, March 23, 1899

Dear friend:

Your communication dated March 20th containing an extract of an address delivered by Dr. von Holst before the students of the University of Chicago I have read with interest, and have pondered over it with sincere earnestness.

I note that Dr. von Holst acknowledges that President Harper, also of the University of Chicago, differs from him in his opinion of the subject "expansion."

In justice to my own feelings on this subject, let me say that there can be no one more liberal as to the liberties of others than I am myself. I feel that all American citizens are entitled to their own opinions and to express them if they feel inclined to do so. That is the blessed liberty that American freedom gives to us all. One of the most beautiful features of the gift of my husband is his insertion among its laws that the purposes of the University are "to promote the public welfare by exercising an influence in behalf of humanity and civilization, teaching the blessings of liberty regulated by law, and inculcating love and reverence

135

for the great principles of government as derived from the inalienable rights of man to life, liberty, and the pursuit of happiness." And this I think should be carried out in a smaller way in the smaller government of the Leland Stanford Junior University.

I consider it a very doubtful question whether or not a president of a university who knows in his heart he is looked up to and worshiped as an ideal man, who has the veneration and love and admiration of its entire body to such an extent that they see no imperfections, whose word is law, whose influence is far beyond his conception, should step outside the bounds of the university itself and campaign ardently, heroically, and unceasingly in favor of an object and to accomplish an end wholly outside of any benefits which may recur in the future to the welfare of the university. When a man assumes to be a leader and campaigner of a vital political issue, he really, in my humble and womanly opinion, oversteps the boundary line of what is expected from a president of a university.

Freedom of thought, freedom of action, freedom of speech as a civilian, as an American citizen, as a teacher, as an exponent of all that is high and noble—no one could feel more earnestly and religiously than I that each one and all possess these rights in their own name and in the liberty which God in His goodness has given to all American citizens.

As you know, my husband was an ardent and earnest Republican. He never flaunted the vices or the mistakes of his party leaders before the public. He praised their virtues and deplored in secret their vices, but he never would have used the president of the great University which he founded to further his political views or his enmities or his prejudices.

And Doctor, I consider the lectures and opinions of a professor secondary to those of a president of a university. Professor Ross, as you know, overstepped the bounds and entered into a political campaign which was as distasteful to you as to me, and both you and I felt Professor Ross had been an injury to the University.

Always your sincere, loyal, and unfaltering friend,

Jane L. Stanford

Despite Dr. Jordan's brave attempts to still the troubled waters, the unfortunate controversy over Professor Ross's outspokenness grew in intensity and on November 11, 1900, President Jordan accepted his long withheld resignation. Ross himself put it more bluntly. "Well, boys, I'm fired," he told a group of student reporters and placed the blame

136

squarely on Mrs. Stanford. Two months later George E. Howard, a professor of history who had strongly supported Dr. Ross, resigned in protest.

Jane Stanford, who had left for Europe before the resignation, was kept fully informed. From the Grand Hotel in Rome she wrote to Dr. Jordan:

Rome, December 14, 1900

Dear friend:

I delayed answering your telegrams—"Turmoil practically over. Faculty with scarcely an exception loyal and true. As for Ross, you were right, not I." and "Howard regrets rash speech; wise to treat him leniently."—taking time to allow the newspapers to arrive that would give me the information I needed as to the unnecessary tumult which had arisen as a consequence of the dismissal of a professor. At this date I think I understand the situation clearly, as on my arrival here, besides a large batch of newspapers, I also received many letters from friends who have given me their impressions and their sympathy, and I also found here your personal letter and those which you had received from others. In conclusion I find the subject too distasteful and too distressing to say any more than I have already said in the past.

In regard to Professor Howard, it could not possibly satisfy you to receive an individual apology when he made his unwarrantable and pernicious address to the students, which was given to the newspapers and reached thousands of people, but he should make his apology through the same source and retract his unchristian attack upon you, myself, my husband, and the University, and even this can not efface the injury that has been done.

In my heart I wish that the world could know from you, as I know, that you thought Prof. Ross "a consummate fool, a miracle of tactlessness," but found "that he was at bottom just a dime novel villain." This really expressed your honest opinion, and it is time the world should know it in order to vindicate and protect the character and the well-being of the University.

I could lay down my life for the University, not for any pride I have in its perpetuating the name of our dear son and ourselves, its founders, but for the sincere hope I cherish in its sending forth to the world grand men and women who will aid in developing the best there is to be found in human nature.

While I have not expressed to you, or to anyone, what I have suffered myself, I will say that I feel the deepest and most heartfelt sympathy for you, and regret the effort that has been made by the newspapers to estrange our relations towards each other. I am ever, as in the past,

Your friend,
Jane L. Stanford

Much as Mrs. Stanford might have wished to forget the Ross affair, she was not allowed to do so.

Shepheard's Hotel, Cairo, January 30, 1901

Dear friend:

Some time has elapsed since my writing to you. Now, as I am on the eve of starting for the long anticipated trip up the Nile and expect to take six weeks or two months, if all goes well, I think it best to acknowledge the receipt of your cablegram received here on January 25th— "Ask permission to publish in University's defense certain passages from your letters as Leib* and I may deem advisable." To be frank with you, I do not feel happy over the fact that you wish again to justify your action by quoting me. I have said nothing in my letters that I would object to have quoted. I am very thankful that I have said so much less than I *feel* in regard to this controversy over Ross. My answer by cable —"I decline being further quoted in the Ross matter. Your personal knowledge of the man is sufficient to defend the University."—expressed to you that I feel it wrong to quote me in my absence.

I am sorry that just on the eve of my departure I am again filled with anxiety in regard to the effect all this controversy may have upon the future of the University.

If my earnest and heartfelt prayers are heard by our dear Savior and all the loved ones, it will end without injury to the cause which is so dear to our hearts. I have not been well in the past few weeks, but I think it is all in consequence of the anxiety and wakeful hours that I have spent over this trouble and I hope the Nile trip will be all I wish for.

I think of you and dear Mrs. Jordan oftener than you dream of. Scarcely a day passes but I feel all it means to you both, and I also include dear Knight, to see the vacant chair, the little playthings, the reminders that never go away, of that dear precious child, and if I could in any way bring comfort to your hearts you can be assured I would willingly make a great sacrifice to do so. But time alone can reconcile

---

* Samuel F. Leib, president, Stanford Board of Trustees.

you, and I do not know that then reconciliation will come. It never has come to me, and never have I missed the strong protection of my dear husband more than I have during this trouble about Ross.

Let me assure you, dear friend, that I sympathize with you in the anxious hours that you must have spent over the insubordination on the part of the professors who have resigned. I must say that I think you will be stronger and have better control over the professors that are left than you have ever had before, for they will realize that there is a supreme head above theirs in the institution, for not one of them has the welfare and future good of the University at heart as you and I have. We are not anxious to promote and advance the professors in the opinion of the public, but we are anxious that they shall send forth grand men and women who have noble aims and high aspirations to benefit humanity.

I am, as ever in the past,

Your earnest friend and
well-wisher,
Jane L. Stanford

During the course of her river journey Jane continued to receive disquieting news about affairs on the campus. In spite of the world clamor those events had caused, she wrote to Dr. Jordan of her belief in the just guidance of a higher power and her steadfast trust in President Jordan's conduct of the University.

Denderhah, on the Nile, Egypt, February 20, 1901

Dear friend:

Since leaving Cairo three weeks ago, I had one mail forwarded to me, and among the letters was yours of January 15th.

In regard to this dreadful affair, which has seemed to disturb the whole world and brought such severe and unjust criticism upon me, I have but this to say. If I had not a sincere and honest belief in a dear, precious, loving Father, who knows all and everything we do and is just in His judgments, if, my dear friend, I did not know this and trust Him to govern and rule the University for its best interests, and know He will guide you if you ask Him, and will guide and support me, I could not have endured the adverse criticism that has come through the dismissal of Professor Ross.

I cannot but feel since this second episode, the resignation of Dr. Howard and the four or five other professors, that the crisis had been brought about by a higher power than any on earth, for it looked to me, from my standpoint, that the professors were not only mutinous but had planned to govern and rule the University independent of its president. It was disloyalty to you who placed them in their positions that, if overlooked, would have been far more disastrous in the end than anything that has yet occurred.

Your past ten years of successful management of the University's affairs entitles you to the deepest respect and sympathy of the faculty in whatever position you might take in regard to the management, and no saying of Dr. Howard or any other professor in the institution can make me falter in my trust, respect, and faith in your ability and your devotion to the blessed work entrusted to your care by my dear husband and myself.

As ever, yours sincerely,
Jane L. Stanford

From Aswan five days later another letter was mailed to Dr. Jordan. Jane Stanford regretted that the few professors who had supported Doctors Ross and Howard had not also been dismissed and praised those who were loyal. "I admire Professor Branner's heroic, manly, and straightforward action in the affair, and this ends all I have to say in regard to the matter."

Abruptly changing the subject, she reported: "I received a telegram from my brother a few days ago saying 'University bills passed both houses Legislature, and were signed by Governor on Friday.' I do not see how they could have done differently, for had these bills not passed, it certainly would have made me feel that the gift by my husband and myself had been thrown at my feet."

Though the news that certain University bills had been passed by the State Legislature and signed by the Governor had been received quite casually by Mrs. Stanford, the event marked the successful conclusion of a vital episode in Stanford history. It dealt with the fortuitous disclosure of the shaky legal foundation on which the University rested and how this had been corrected by the passage of an amendment to the State Constitution. This was achieved by the devotion and hard work of a group of Stanford's young alumni led by George E. Crothers, a member of the Pioneer Class and among the early graduates of the University's law department. By rare good fortune he had met Mrs. Stanford in the spring of 1898. She saw in him a physical resemblance to her son and, instinctively recognizing his worth, gave him her full confidence. As a result he became one of her closest friends and advisors. With her full cooperation Crothers studied the financial and legal status of the University minutely and was invaluable in helping to untangle the legal web in which it was enmeshed, and for which he refused any recompense except that of being named a University Trustee, the first alumnus and youngest person to be selected. Mrs. Stanford's role in all this, though important, had been passive and she had wisely remained above the fray. Her correspondence makes no further mention of this significant event.

In another quick change of pace financial consideration again took over the lead. Thinking things over during quiet days on the Nile, between the bursts of explosive news from home, Jane had come to the firm conclusion to limit the number of students and not allow an increase to eat up the interest at her disposal. More students would also mean additions to the faculty. "It is quality, not quantity that I am anxious to obtain." The blow was therefore all the greater when she received Jordan's cable. "Have asked in second letter two hundred thirty thousand next salary roll. Very important."

The letters mentioned were waiting for her on her return to Cairo. Jane was in full agreement with Jordan's view that weak places on the faculty needed strengthening: "If we had had more strong, upright, honorable men we would never have been called upon to pass through the crisis we did. I have come to the conclusion that the professors who have already left were prepared to take possession of the University and manage it according to their own desires. From all I have read of the opinions of the dissatisfied part of the faculty, there are still remaining enough to breed rebellion against the present administration, but I think you understand the situation fully and will make strong, weak places."

Shortly afterward, in a somewhat unusual expansive mood and influenced perhaps by her surroundings, Jane cabled to Dr. Jordan from Jerusalem: "For your happiness grant two hundred thirty thousand." Two days later, however, she had changed her mind. "Take no action on salary question. Desire to reconsider. Need more information." A cautionary cable from her brother, who probably knew her financial situation and that of the University even better than she did, had caused her to retract her earlier offer. In a follow-up letter she gave Dr. Jordan the reason for her vacillation.

Jerusalem, April 9, 1901

Kind friend:

I hasten to explain the cause of my reconsidering the cable message sent you, one consenting to an increase of $18,000, making the salary roll $225,000, and a second message consenting to a further increase of $5,000, making the total $230,000. It was a spontaneous effort on my part to make you happy and forget the unpleasant notoriety that has been attached to the dismissal of Professor Ross.

I was brought to a realizing sense of my hastiness by a cable message from my brother. He is thoroughly well acquainted with my resources, even to the last dollar, and knows full well what a large expenditure of money I am calling for during this present year and coming year for buildings which are going up and which have to be equipped. When I seriously think of the indebtedness which I shall have to meet, I am quite nervous and anxious, for I never intend to spend any of the principal; in fact, I am practicing economy to the fullest extent on all my travels, fearing that I might be profligate with money that is needed to pay for the buildings.

In a way I have endeavored, as far as possible, to shake off from my mind business affairs. Indeed if I heeded them, I should feel it my duty to be at home at present, on account of some business that needs my attention at the Pacific Improvement Company. I have learned through experience that my brother, while in hearty sympathy and accord with all my wishes concerning the University and its future, has to check me occasionally and remind me that I have not the Bank of England to draw upon.

After two or three wakeful nights, mortified that I had to retract, I concluded to have you give my brother your confidence, telling him your wants and your needs, and he to be guided by what he knows of my money affairs in regard to further allowance that can be made this year. I would not embarrass him by being rash and making promises that cannot be fulfilled, which I fear would be the case were I to accede to the sudden and unexpected large increase over last year in the faculty salary roll.

Yours sincerely,
Jane L. Stanford

Despite all Jane's attempts to bury it, the ghost of the Ross affair kept reappearing. From Marseilles on April 26 she wrote to Dr. Jordan:

"To be as brief as possible, I will only allude to the suggestion made by you that I write to Mr. Hamlin in regard to the Ross incident. The Ross affair in itself was not of much import, if it had been conducted properly, which it was not. I hope that you will now consider it concluded, and in answer to your letter I cabled you the following: 'Consider Ross matter concluded and not discuss it. I am firm in saying nothing.' And I shall say nothing to Mr. Hamlin. . . ."

The heat of the Ross affair had begun to dissipate, and, although it simmered along for several years, its effects finally faded entirely.

In spite of Jane's desire to return promptly to Palo Alto at the conclusion of her European tour, a physical disability detained her in New York. A surgeon had removed seven wens from Mrs. Stanford's scalp and the wounds had been slow in healing. She described her ordeal to Dr. Jordan in graphic detail and assured him she had not had a "funny" time.

The new year found a disconsolate Jane Stanford still in New York. When she at last was home again, money matters once more came to the fore and this time Jane was happy to be able to comply with the requested salary roll. She was distressed, however, at Dr. Jordan's intimation that the University had not reached the high standard for which she had hoped.

Palo Alto, March 24, 1902

Dear Sir:

Your letter of today has just been read. I learn that you require $230,650 which will be sufficient for your salary roll this year. I am very glad indeed that I am able to concede to your wish, for I always want you to understand that under no consideration would I make you feel that you are limited and I am withholding the means which you consider absolutely necessary for the advancement of the work under your care.

I must confess, however, that your letter of February 6th was very discouraging. After all that has been done and the vast amount that has been expended, we are only a "college." It seemed to me, for a few days after I had received this letter, that we had better lower our aspirations and keep it to a first class school, without even attempting to call it a college, let alone a university, for I fear with all the means at command for the purpose of educating young men and women, there will never be sufficient in the future to bring it up to the standard I fondly dream of. To know this institution is on such a low plane has actually made me sick.

I am very pleased indeed to know that Professor and Mrs. Smith are to return. They were always favorites of mine, for both of them in their way are very superior.

143

Although not familiarizing myself with the various professors and their accomplishments, I find to my surprise that the measure of them all has been pretty well taken by the public and the students, and I have, through their knowledge, been kept well informed of the status of them all.

Yours respectfully,
Jane L. Stanford

An unforeseen situation of a totally different nature greatly distressed Mrs. Stanford. The Founding Grant had set aside about ten acres in the arboretum as a burying place for persons connected with the University. In time this provision brought disturbing consequences and Mrs. Stanford asked that the privilege be rescinded and sent the president of the Board of Trustees, Samuel F. Leib, a letter and resolution to that effect.

Palo Alto, July 9, 1902

Kind friend:

The enclosed I send to you for future use. I have been pained so often in the past, and at present, by being applied to for permission to bury in the Arboretum distant relatives of those connected with the Leland Stanford Jr. University as teachers, and, fully realizing what it will mean in years to come if such requests are granted, I have concluded the cemetery shall now be closed forever, and no further burials allowed. . . .

Another reason why I take this stand is because of the really disgraceful condition of some of the graves of the once loved ones who have been placed there by professors of the institution. Only ten acres were set aside for burial purposes, and no money was ever expected to be used to keep these graves in order; and in years hence ten acres would be filled with the dead and an eyesore, as it is already.

I feel assured I am right in the decision I have made not to allow any more burials in the present cemetery; neither can any more burials be made on any of the land belonging to the said University. It will be painful to me to have to bear the adverse criticism that I will be subjected to when this resolve is made public, but, when my heart and my soul tell me I am doing right and the very thing of all things my husband would do were he here in my place and had experienced what I have, I have the courage to act.

With highest respect, I remain as of old,
Your friend,
Jane L. Stanford

Jane was at constant pains to balance University expense against income and was distressed that the amount of money originally intended for buildings had already been far exceeded and was convinced that a halt had to be called somewhere. She closely followed all new construction, personally inspecting the buildings as the work progressed, and continued her scrutiny while they were being equipped.

Her overall view of professors may have been somewhat clouded by the invective she had sustained in the long drawn out controversy over Professor Ross. "In my visit lately through the new buildings I find the professors have yielded to extravagances which might have been avoided, and I do not like it. I do not like to have any professor visiting The City and selecting goods, and getting prices on some, which I have to pay for, and I have given my brother instructions to buy everything himself, and only plain necessities, in the future."

Occupancy of the new buildings became a further matter of controversy. As the structures were completed, Mrs. Stanford feared that the Inner Quadrangle would be deserted entirely because so many professors seemed anxious to move into new quarters. She thought she had been anticipating future needs and was surprised to learn that every fresh space was to be occupied. "I cannot but feel that in some instances professors should be content with their old quarters. Of course I do not mean the overcrowded class such as Prof. Stillman had and Dr. Branner. . . . Some professors discipline themselves, and some are under no discipline and do not themselves discipline the assistants or students under them. I like to see a spirit of satisfaction. If everyone is to spread out and leave the old quarters to go to new ones, I fear the stone age will not be over with for some time."

Jane Stanford's early struggle to keep the University alive had taught her the value of thrift and this had been reinforced by a visit to the University of Tokyo, where she had been greatly impressed by the remarkable accomplishments obtained with limited means. A letter from its president had reminded her of this and she hastened to give Dr. Jordan her views.

San Francisco, February 19, 1903

Dear friend:

When in Tokyo I visited the University of which Mr. E. Kamada is the president. I have just received the enclosed letter to remind me of my promise made when there. In speaking of sending publications from our University I in reality meant to assist with their law library. They had but a handful of books—not more than 200—and the great work done there surprised and pleased me. Everything is on such a plain, sensible plan. It touched me very deeply, the comparison between that institution of 1,700 students with a less number at our University—less comforts, no extravagance, everything simple to a degree that was astonishing—only the necessities, no money spent except for positive and actual necessaries.

I volunteered under the inspiration of the feeling to assist them in their admirable and grand work by enlarging the law library. Mr. Kamada mistook my purpose, as you see by the copy of letter enclosed. It has occurred to me that if you would send them back numbers of our public register books, copies of *Quad*, *Sequoia*, and surplus publications such as are not needed for our students, it would enlighten them as to our course of study and how we carry on the work here, which I know would be pleasant for them to have. For the past two months I have been looking for law books to add to their meager library but have failed as yet to accomplish anything, so have come to the conclusion to send a check and let them buy the much needed books, and which to them will seem a great Godsend. . . .

Truly yours,
Jane L. Stanford

20

"To the glory of God this Church was conceived."

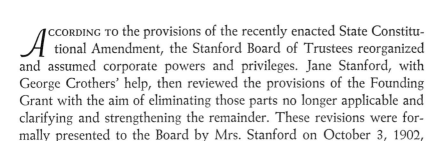

*A*CCORDING TO the provisions of the recently enacted State Constitutional Amendment, the Stanford Board of Trustees reorganized and assumed corporate powers and privileges. Jane Stanford, with George Crothers' help, then reviewed the provisions of the Founding Grant with the aim of eliminating those parts no longer applicable and clarifying and strengthening the remainder. These revisions were formally presented to the Board by Mrs. Stanford on October 3, 1902, and were approved unanimously.

In the light of recent disturbing events, she went into some detail about the ethical principles on which the institution was founded: "The University must be forever maintained upon a strictly nonpartisan and nonsectarian basis. It must never become an instrument in the hands of any political party or any religious sect or organization. . . . I desire that the University shall forever be kept out of politics, and that no professor shall electioneer among or seek to dominate other professors or the students for the success of any political party or candidate in any political contest. I hope that every voter, whether professor or student, will always thoroughly inform himself upon every principle involved, and as to the merits of every candidate seeking his suffrage, and then vote according to his own best judgment and conscience, irrespective of any importunity of others. . . ."

Her views on equality were delineated: "The University has been endowed with a view of offering instruction free, or nearly free, that it may resist the tendency to the stratification of society, by keeping open an avenue whereby the deserving and exceptional may rise through their own efforts from the lowest to the highest stations in life. A spirit of equality must accordingly be maintained within the University. To this end it shall be the duty of the University authorities to prohibit excessive expenditures and other excesses on the part of students, and the formation or growth of any organization, custom, or social function that tends to the development of exclusive or undemocratic castes within the University, and to exclude from the institution anyone whose conduct is inconsistent with the spirit of the foundation."

Always in the forefront of Jane Stanford's mind was the essential place religion should hold in the education of youth; yet it must be voluntary on the student's part and inspired by example, not rote. The keystone of this goal was the Memorial Church. Shortly before its completion it was visited by the president of the University of California, Benjamin Ide Wheeler, who wrote:

Berkeley, September 25, 1902

Dear Mrs. Stanford:

I had today the great pleasure of visiting the new chapel which you have added to the resources of Stanford University, and I cannot forbear sending you a word of thanks in behalf of interests I represent for this great good you have done the state. It is a direct contribution to the influences which make for good in the great community of which we are all members. As the generations pass through this building they will be uplifted and inspired toward better and larger living, and all of us and all our institutions that strive toward bettering human life will share the blessing.

Very sincerely yours,
Benj. I. Wheeler

To which Jane Stanford promptly replied:

Highly prized friend:

I cannot express the great satisfaction which it was to me to receive the words of commendation which you have bestowed upon the work so dear to my soul—the building and beautifying of the Church, in which in a feeble way I have endeavored to tell the beautiful story of the life of the Son of God, our precious Savior. To the glory of God this Church was conceived, and worked out with a fervent and prayerful reverence of His holy name. It has indeed been a work of love. In thinking of it and the University at large, I cannot but feel that the education which the students are receiving is secondary, if a religious and spiritual influence is not exerted over them all to develop the soul germ which lies dormant in so many, and which is for their ultimate good, not only here but hereafter.

The Church is, as in my own mind I think it, the Kohinoor in the setting of the entire institution, and I cannot express how much it is to me to receive your sympathy, your sustaining and strengthening thoughts, and your helpfulness and support in this undertaking to teach Christ and His beautiful life through the influence of this Church.

I pray that God will bless you for your kind act and kind words.

Most sincerely yours,
Jane L. Stanford

Jane held that science and scholarship were useful tools for a man's betterment but his greater need was character. While acknowledging that all studies, if taken seriously, were uplifting, she thought that institutions and educators spent too little time on moral and spiritual instruction.

Next to President Jordan among the faculty, Dr. Branner, professor of geology, was closest to her and she often expressed to him her views on education and life. The University tried to fit men for professions, she said, but ignored the fact that no one wanted to employ a man who lacked sound principles, no matter how much he might know about some particular subject. Reputedly only students of good character were admitted to the University, but she did not believe enough effort was made to ascertain that quality beforehand and that no amount of learning could take the place of decency. "That, Mr. Branner," Jane declared, "is why I am so much more interested in the Church on the campus than I am in your precious rocks."

She was aware of the complaint by some that the library should have occupied the central position on which the Church stands, but she rejected this. "Like any other force, education needs intelligent guidance if it is to serve any good purpose." And so, flanked by classrooms but rising above them, Memorial Church overlooks the Inner Quadrangle, and the morning sun illumines its façade and the mosaic of exquisite Italian artistry depicting the Savior speaking to His disciples. In the cloister bronze plaques set in squares of the pathway mark the year of each passing class—milestones for one task well done and the beginning of new adventures.

True to her beliefs, Jane Stanford was a churchgoer but the denominations she attended varied. Catholicism had a strong appeal, perhaps nurtured by the devoted attention of the Sisters of Florence during her son's fatal illness, but she did not join the church. She knew and admired Pope Leo XIII, and he helped select some of the Biblical scenes which add so much to the beauty of Memorial Church.

Jane kept a notebook and jotted down appealing sayings she read or heard and these she paraphrased in her own words. A number of them are carved in the stone walls in the interior of the Church. One in the East Transept reads:

> Religion is intended as a comfort, a solace, a necessity to the soul's welfare; and whichever form of religion furnishes the greatest comfort, the greatest solace it is the form which should be adopted, be its name what it will.
>
> The best form of religion is trust in God and a firm belief in the immortality of the soul, life everlasting.

Memorial Church was dedicated on January 25, 1903, by its distinguished pastor, Dr. Heber Newton, formerly rector of All Souls Church in New York City. Several hundred chairs were added to supplement the seating for 1,800 in the regular pews, and all were filled when the doors were closed promptly at eleven on that memorable Sunday morning. The students had entered in groups from opposite sides of the Church, guided by forty student ushers. Among the dignitaries from a wide surrounding area were churchmen of every denomination, educators, and Trustees of the University. Benjamin Ide Wheeler was the special guest of President Jordan. Jane Stanford was accompanied by her brother, Charles G. Lathrop, and Captain N.T. Smith, the longtime friend and associate of the late Senator.

True to Mrs. Stanford's wishes, the services were conducted in a nonsectarian manner. Dr. Newton spoke in moving language of the great churches of the world of all creeds and times, in which narrow minds would note their differences but in which "Deeper natures will see in each of these great churches, as in the types of thought and feeling they express, something to admire, to sympathize with, to stir a sense of community life, to knot more closely the sacred bonds of human fellowship. . . ."

At intervals a choir of one hundred voices, which had been practicing for a year under organist Scott Brook, filled the great church with joyful harmony.

During the afternoon service Rev. David Charles Gardner spoke of the part religion might play in education. "Here in the inauguration of this work is the recognition of religion as a principle in the culture and education of men. . . . Here by the western shore of the New World, the theater of the drama of the future, we begin a unique experiment. No less an experiment than this: To test whether a nonsectarian Church can minister to the spiritual needs of a great University. . . ."

Most significant perhaps was the feeling of youth itself, which was summed up in an editorial of the student paper, then called *The Daily Palo Alto*, or more affectionately the "Dippy." "The spiritual needs of the University will be administered to through a nonsectarian church. There will be no creed, no bishopric, no polity, no ecclesiastical ordinances or diocese. . . . Generation after generation of students will arrive on the campus, imbibe large draughts of the Stanford spirit, and go forth into the world men and women better able to see things, hear things, and do things."

Shortly after the dedication Dr. Newton resigned. Seemingly he could not catch the free spirit of the West. For one thing, he wished to hire at considerable expense a professional choralist from his former church, but this was neither Jane Stanford's nor the Rev. Dr. Gardner's idea of community participation. The latter then assumed the religious leadership of the Stanford community under the modest title of chaplain. It was a happy sequence, for David Charles Gardner endeared himself to all and served until 1936.

On receipt of a memorial sermon delivered by Dr. Gardner a year after the dedication, Jane wrote to him from Cairo:

Cairo, February 26, 1904

Christian friend:

The memorial sermon delivered by you on January 24th has reached me. I have carefully read it through and enjoy thinking of all you have said on the occasion. One point which has impressed me very deeply is the fact that you had the courage to speak openly and frankly in regard to the responsibility that rests upon the members of the faculty as to whether or not they set an example of respect for the teachings of the Church of which you are the pastor. The members of the faculty can very greatly help to make religion become popular at the University. A religious air pervades the Church, at least. I endeavored to make the edifice sacred by beautifying it with statues of the holy family and Christ's Apostles, with mosaic pictures relating to the life of our precious Savior and stories told in the old Bible. I did this to impress the students and to aid the preacher in doing the work among precious souls, seeking for light for which we earnestly pray. Without teaching a belief in God and His beloved Son and life beyond this on Earth, the University fails in its most vital importance. . . .

How little my dear ones and I realized the awful responsibilities we took upon our poor weak selves when we formed the project of benefiting humanity. I realize fully at this late day that education of the brain is not all that God exacts from us. The soul life and high moral sense must be awakened and book learning is not all that is required.

I think my loved ones, in a sense, are holding me very responsible for an influence to better conditions, and not to allow parents to feel that they are sending their loved ones to a Godless institution. The gift was to God and to humanity to enlighten men and women as to their holiest obligations towards Him who doeth all things well, and if the University fails to do this, we have not done our work well, and not what was expected by the Giver of all.

Your friend and well wisher,
Mrs. Leland Stanford

21

The Trustees Take the Helm

DURING APRIL 1903 there was a serious outbreak of typhoid fever on the campus and in Palo Alto. About 120 students were afflicted and eight died. Prompt action by the Palo Alto Board of Health in locating and sealing the source of the infection in two nearby dairies and untiring care by doctors and nurses, many of the latter student volunteers, promptly contained what might have become a major epidemic. There was no panic and the University work continued without interruption.

The epidemic focused attention on health hazards at the University and available means of treatment. During the early years there were few physicians and there was no hospital in the area. In 1895 a Students' Guild was formed to provide health care for a fee of fifty cents per person each semester. The need for a hospital was recognized but the funds were not available. Mrs. Stanford realized that an accessible hospital was a necessity but objected to one on the campus and was opposed to having outside interests in control of any building on University grounds. She stated to Dr. Jordan: "I intend to make arrangements myself for a hospital off the campus and to be under the control of a physician entirely disinterested, without any responsibility ensuing upon the Trustees for the maintenance thereof. I feel very decided on the subject. There must not be a hospital on the campus."

The emergency proved a boon to the Guild. Five thousand dollars was collected and half as much more contributed by Mrs. Stanford. A building was rented in Palo Alto and made into a hospital, while on the campus a part of Encina Hall was so used. Whether the latter constituted a temporary hospital or not seems equivocal. Jane Stanford apparently did not think so: "I learned from Mr. Addison last evening that there were no patients in Encina Hall except the four who are occupying rooms there," she wrote to Dr. Jordan. "He tells me they are attended by two nurses. I have given instructions not to take any sick ones in from outside the Hall. As there are over 200 students occupying rooms there, it certainly would be a fatal mistake to convert the dormitory into a temporary hospital. It's a great relief to my mind to find the facts as they are."

In May of the same critical year, with the peak of the contagion over, Jane Stanford asked Dr. Jordan to deliver an invitation to all Stanford students. Though nothing could ever lessen the depth of her own feeling over the loss of her son, she did not want to inflict her sad recollections on the young people she had grown to love so dearly. The garden party she planned for them was to be on the thirty-fifth anniversary of Leland Stanford Jr.'s birthday. Her invitation read:

"Wishing this year the students of the Leland Stanford Junior University to vary the manner of commemorating my son's birthday, I present my compliments to the entire student body of ladies and gentlemen, and cordially invite them to a garden fete on my private grounds at Stanford, on Friday, May 14th, 1903, from three to six o'clock.

"Only students expected.

"Dancing."

On May 18, 1903, four days after the party and thirteen days before she was to resign her powers as surviving founder of the University, Jane Stanford sent a critical communication to President Jordan in which she took full advantage of the sweeping power she still possessed under the provisions of the Founding Grant. After deliberating long and carefully over his statement outlining University requirements for the coming year, she noted with great surprise that he had already engaged new professors and assistants without having discussed the matter with her, or asking her if she could afford the additional expense. "Instead of allowing you a 'free hand' and 'to use your best discretion for the salary roll,' I think it is absolutely necessary for me to use my best discretion, as probably I know better what I can afford than anyone else, and I alone am responsible for the payment of obligations." She reiterated her determination to complete and equip the necessary buildings before enlarging the student body and faculty and to do this without borrowing.

Another matter disturbed Jane: "There is one thing that troubles me very much, this constant comparison of our University with Berkeley, Harvard, Yale, Cornell, etc. These all have behind them the support of states and wealthy citizens and rich students. Every citizen of our state is taxed to support the Berkeley university, as you know, and I do not think there is a citizen in our state who is taxed more heavily than I am to support that institution, as my taxes alone amount to $35,000 a year. . . .

"Always remember we are simply a unique institution of our own; not trying to compete with any other in the world, simply with God's blessing, giving to the young a useful mental and manual education to help them through life, and whatever else all other institutions may be able to accomplish through the help of greater means than we command, we are simply not vying or envying or trying to outdo anyone. We are simply our own selves, doing the best we can with the means that God has given me to carry on the good work. I have never needed to be urged, for I endeavor to do the best I can the few years remaining to me."

With the dedication of Memorial Church, Jane Stanford considered her work completed and, fearing that her seventy-five years and failing health might impair her judgment, she told George Crothers that everyone's interests would be served best if she relinquished her powers as surviving founder and transferred all authority to the Trustees and their successors forever. This she did in her last address to the Board on June 1, 1903.

The meeting took place in the study of her San Francisco home, where eighteen years before Leland and she presented the Founding Grant of Stanford University to its appointed Trustees. During the proceedings Jane's fear that her judgment might be failing came dangerously close to being proven correct. Doubtless influenced by some disparaging reports about the behavior of a few men and women students on the University grounds, Jane, in a supplementary statement which she had not shown to Crothers, suggested to the Trustees that if they should ever conclude that coeducation was a failure, they should abolish it. George Crothers adroitly asked for a short recess. Taking Mrs. Stanford aside, he pointed out that the Trustees could not take the step she proposed without a change in the Founding Grant, and persuaded her not to take such a fateful step. She thereupon said she would allow the trust to stand and then read her letter resigning her powers. It was accepted by the Trustees, who immediately made her a fellow member and their president.

A month later, as one final safeguard against possible future suits, a legal determination of the validity of all pertinent documents was carried out at a special hearing before the Superior Court in the County of Santa Clara. The confirmatory decree was issued and signed by Judge M.H. Hyland on July 3, 1903.

In August Jane left on an around-the-world trip which included a visit with Senator Stanford's brother, Thomas Welton Stanford, in Australia. With responsibilities no longer dogging her footsteps at every turn, she was better able to enjoy each new scene and event, and her letters became fewer. From Colombo, Ceylon, on October 30, 1903, she wrote to Dr. Jordan giving her felicitations on the expected addition to his family.

Coeducation had been a settled policy at Stanford from the beginning, with only that one hazardous moment, happily averted, just before Mrs. Stanford had offered her resignation to the Board of Trustees. However, the subject came up again from a different source after her return from abroad. Susan L. Mills, president of Mills College, the well-known school for women in Oakland, California, sought Mrs. Stanford's views on this important issue.

"... The matter concerning which I wished to talk with you was in regard to coeducation. We both believe in it—at the same time our practice is different—but the general sentiment of the community here and at the East is changing, and it is thought better that young men and young women during their undergraduate work should not be taught together. It was concerning this whole subject that I thought I would like to talk with you after your long experience and observation.

"I have a great horror of appearing in print in any way, and so I am very careful as to what I write. I know you will appreciate my feeling. Some time possibly you will feel that you have the leisure so that I can have a quiet talk with you. ..."

Mrs. Stanford's reply to Susan Mills came from the Hotel Del Monte.

Monterey, California; July 14, 1904

Dear Mrs. Mills:

Coeducation is in my feeble opinion an unsolved question. It is still in its infancy, and only time and experience can definitely settle the very important and very serious question.

I am willing to give it a fair and impartial trial, and I believe God, who in His wisdom knows all—even in sorrow as well as in joy—will open the minds of the wise rulers of earth to decide this troublesome and delicate question, and it will be in the end settled to the advantage of both sexes.

The Trustees of the Stanford University are wise, experienced men, some of them university graduates, and they are giving me great release from responsibility that had grown too heavy from its long protracted term; and growing older each year, not younger, made me feel it was time to ask these grand men to help me. They have responded most nobly and the outlook is proving far beyond my fondest expectations.

> With friendly greetings,
> your well-wisher,
> Jane L. Stanford

At home Jane was soon again concerned with University problems, though the responsibility of their solution was no longer hers alone. She could not refrain from expressing her hurt at what appeared to be Dr. Jordan's lack of understanding in a matter on which she felt so deeply.

Palo Alto; September 10, 1904

Dear Dr. Jordan:

I was quite surprised to find that any ceremony was expected in laying the cornerstone of the new library. I should very much prefer to have it done without any ado of any kind. I prefer to do what is to be done in a quiet, unpretentious, unsensational manner. I have often wished that I could by a thought raise up the buildings as a mushroom grows in one night. One of the pleasures of adding to and beautifying the buildings is to do it without the blowing of trumpets, and surprise the students by an added gem here and there which will complete the whole in symmetry and perfection as my husband intended.

I was very sorry indeed to notice in a little article in our local paper that in your address the allusion was made again to the "stone age," and that (when it was over, which it would be in a short time) such promises were made to the students as would lead them to think that they were on the eve of a new rebirth as to expansion and growth, for you cannot have forgotten the impression which I have endeavored to give you, that the growth will be slow and the numbers not increased as to students, nor as to professors. And it will be the policy of the Trustees and myself to develop quality rather than quantity; and these promises to the students, which are alluring, are placing us all, in a way, in a false position, which I deplore.

I have referred to this subject of the "stone age" because it has hurt my feelings in that it has given me the impression that you have not all this time been in sympathy and accord with my putting up such extensive and expensive buildings which I myself considered my duty and it has afforded me great pleasure; and even when these buildings are completed, and less of the income used for such purposes, still it is our intention to husband the income and not spend all each year for educational purposes.

It is, I think, the firm intention of the Trustees to lay aside every year a certain amount which can never be used for any purpose except to let it accumulate and reinforce the interest for an emergency which might occur in depreciation of values and destruction of buildings.*

> Your friend,
> Jane L. Stanford

Patiently, the very next day, Dr. Jordan wrote to allay her misgivings.

Stanford University, September 11, 1904

My dear friend:

I do not think that you would have objected to what I actually said to the students. I have made it very clear to professors and students that we do not look forward to large numbers nor to a great variety and range of departments, but to making our teaching in all departments as excellent as the buildings are. My ideal—like yours—has been a relatively small number of graduates—each one thoroughly trained.

I am in the fullest sympathy with the plan of putting up the buildings first and building them as they should be.

I am also in fullest sympathy with the plan of setting aside a large sum each year—perhaps $200,000—to be added to the principal. And

---

* The value of Jane Stanford's foresight in saving for emergencies was amply demonstrated by the catastrophic destruction caused by the great earthquake a year after her death.

I have been very patient (for me) with the necessary limitations in this period of building.

But it is my duty to look after the weak places in the University and I know—and our older students know—that the professors are working under great difficulties. In many cases, the apparatus intended for twenty students has served for fifty and is worn out. There are many subjects taught in all other universities which we do not teach for lack of men or lack of books, and which we send our students elsewhere to get. I do look forward to the time when the teaching here will be the best on earth. I do not wish to see many students—nor even many departments, but I hope that all of these may be made thoroughly efficient.

We are doing today better undergraduate teaching than any other American college, but this can be greatly improved and at no very large additional expense.

I am sure that you and I have exactly the same final purpose in these matters. It is my official duty to watch the small needs and to plan the means of teaching.

For this reason I am sure that I always seem to be reaching for or asking for something new. But the University must always keep growing and growth with us does not mean increase in numbers but in doing things in better ways, and with a broader outlook on what education should mean.

Very truly yours,
David S. Jordan

Soon Jane was greatly enjoying a trip East, and in a relaxed and expansive mood described it to Dr. Jordan in a letter from the Waldorf-Astoria.

New York, December 4, 1904

Dear friend:

It was a great pleasure to me to receive from the alumni the good news of the victory of the Stanford boys in their game with Berkeley. A committee, consisting of three, brought the news in person, but as I was out for the evening they left a very, I might say, affectionate note, imparting their joy and their kind feelings toward myself.

I had hoped to be home before this time, but pressing private business, which developed within the last two weeks, keeps me longer than I expected. To while away the time, pending an engagement which called me here for this special day of the month, I have visited Yale and Harvard, spending a week between the two places. Within a few days I received a letter from President Eliot expressing the greatest personal interest in our work. After having visited the library and gymnasium at Harvard I made an effort to see President Eliot, but found he was in Boston attending a very important meeting of trustees of the university. The next day I returned to New York, and he, finding my card, made a special trip to Boston and called at the Berkeley Hotel to see me, and finding I had just left there, caused him to write me the letter which I prize so highly. I find he is as anxious to meet me as I am to meet him again, and I may go by way of Boston when returning home in order to satisfy a longing I have for a little reminiscence of the past with him. I also have a very kind letter from President Hadley, which I value highly.

After leaving New Haven I visited Norwich, Conn., the birthplace of my father, grandfather, and great-grandfather. You probably know that John Lathrop (my great-grandfather) was the minister of Old South Church in Boston who preached the sermon in that church inciting his hearers to throw the tea overboard in the Boston Harbor. The 200th [sic] anniversary of this event was celebrated two years ago in the new Old South Church in Boston, and his sermon was read on the occasion, and his portrait hangs in this church. I have a portrait of him in the Memorial Room connected with the Museum.

I seemed to have the time to carry out this long wished for visit, and it happened that I was in Norwich on Thanksgiving day and was invited by the two oldest members of the Lathrop family in Norwich to take tea with them. They are fourth cousins of mine and I did not know they existed, but, the papers having announced my arrival, they called upon me and made known their relationship. I did not hesitate to accept their invitation. They live in an old colonial home built over a hundred years ago, filled with beautiful old mahogany furniture, silver, and china. Two sisters live together, both spinsters, one 70 the other 72 years old, grand women of the old school.

The sisters invited five of the oldest townspeople to meet me in the evening, also the minister whose church I attended in the morning and his assistant. It was one of the most memorable evenings of my life, and I feel so grateful to my dear Heavenly Father that He gives me the health, the spirit, and brings about the circumstances which help to make my life enjoyable. Having met these two grand women, so full of intellect, so grand in the position they hold at Norwich, their activity and dignified demeanor as hostesses, has left an impression upon me that I shall never forget.

I am glad that your sister has arrived and is able to take the responsibility of household affairs from Mrs. Jordan's mind.

Yours sincerely,
Jane L. Stanford

Jane Stanford continued to be disturbed over the reported improper behavior of some young men and women on the campus. In a letter to Dr. Jordan she deplored the lack of supervision in the girls' dormitory, Roble Hall, and at the sorority houses.

New York, December 1904

Dear friend:

As a general rule I do not take notice of anonymous communications, and I have received quite a number in relation to the affair mentioned in the enclosed one sent by a "troubled mother." The troubled mother's signature touched my heart, and I would be unfaithful to my conscience were I to cast this into the wastebasket.

Just before I left home I was shocked by having the following said to me in regard to one of the young ladies who graduated from the University last year. The young lady's mother remarked to a lady friend of mine that she was thankful indeed for the education which her daughter had received at the University, but had she a dozen daughters more she would not send another one to Stanford University, as the license allowed them and the disinterested manner in which the young girls were treated as regards their intercourse with young men made her constantly fear some terrible scandal, and this was the reason for the above remark.

I have, in a casual manner, mentioned to you my anxiety about the girls in Roble, but I will now take this opportunity to say that I have for a long while been very uneasy about the management of Roble. I have been convinced that the young woman who acts as matron there knows but little of the usages of good society. I think her faithful, willing, and self-respecting, but more than that is wanted to make young unsophisticated girls under her charge obey the commonplace rules of good breeding. Even more than this is required. The girls should be taught to be circumspect and self-governed in all their conduct. There should be an experienced woman at the head of Roble Hall with some worldly wisdom, who can advise the girls in many ways and impress upon them the indelicacy of seeing young men except in the parlor and in the presence of others and at stated times, not at any and all times as I understand is the fashion in Roble at present. The free and familiar intercourse between the young men and young women students permitted in Roble Hall (which is supposed by the public to be under our supervision) has caused me much anxiety for the last few years. In a certain sense we should be held responsible for the girls' good conduct there.

I am also troubled about the girls in the fraternity houses, as I understand that they are quite lawless and free in their social relations with the young men. I wish there were fewer girls' fraternities on the campus, and hope the limit has been reached, for they seem to be beyond control. You may feel otherwise, and, if you do feel that you have the right to dictate to them in regard to their intercourse with the men students, I hope most sincerely that you will take it upon yourself to assert your right. We may be held responsible by many a troubled mother, while at heart we desire only the best, the purest, and the highest good for the troubled mother's daughter, and we must aim to gain the confidence of all the mothers by a strict surveillance, a high code of social demeanor that will insure the confidence of the public. You and I are already aware that many things have happened that we pray God may never happen again.

Ever yours sincerely,
Jane L. Stanford

Mrs. Stanford agreed with Dr. Jordan's suggestion that memorial services on what he named Founders' Day be held in the Stanford Church, but again stated categorically that only services of a religious nature should ever be held there.

San Francisco, December 28, 1904

Dear Sir:

I have no objection whatever to having the memorial services you desire to hold March 9th, which you call Founders' Day. It seems to me it would be very appropriate indeed to have the services held in the Church built to his, my husband's memory, but under no conditions whatever would I wish it to be simply a secular service. An ordained minister should be invited to speak, as he ordinarily would from the pulpit.

I wish it understood now and forever more that the Church never can be used for any secular purpose whatever. There are sufficient buildings spacious enough to seat large audiences—either the old Chapel or the Assembly Hall—for secular purposes. If it would be arranged to have an ordained minister to speak on that day and appropriate music, it would be fitting and circumspect to have the services held in the Church. If not, the memorial services must be held in the Chapel or Assembly Hall. One transgression in the use of the Church for any other purpose would be a violation of my heretofore and at present expressed directions.

Yours respectfully,
Mrs. Leland Stanford

22

Jane's Last Journey

―――◆―――

*W*HILE AT HER San Francisco home in January 1905, Jane Stanford had a distressing experience. She customarily kept a bottle of Poland water on her bedside table and on sipping it one night detected an unusual bitter taste, a fact confirmed by her secretary and maid. Having rid herself at once of what little she had taken, she suffered no ill effect beyond the momentary disagreeable taste. No immediate concern was felt, but next morning the bottle was taken to Wakelee's drug store for inspection.

Meanwhile, Jane went to one of her favorite spots, the Hotel Vendome in San Jose. After a short stay she returned and was met at the station by Mr. Wilson, Judge Leib, and her brother, who advised her they had engaged rooms for her at the St. Francis Hotel in San Francisco. Analysis of the Poland water had shown that it contained strychnine, but an exhaustive investigation of all the circumstances had failed to reveal anyone's willful wrongdoing. However, her home was still under strict surveillance.

Understandably, Jane Stanford was extremely upset and firmly believed that someone had tried to poison her. The incident cast a pall over her few remaining days. Thinking she might feel safer and recover more quickly in totally new surroundings, she sailed for Honolulu on the steamer *Korea* on February 15, 1905, accompanied by her secretary and a maid.

The day before leaving, with characteristic determination and in spite of her troubled situation, Jane wrote an address for the laying of the cornerstone of the new library. This ran counter to her previously expressed wish to avoid all ceremony on such occasions. That it was directed to the students and was to be read by one of them may help explain the apparent inconsistency. It told of her goals in building Stanford University and of her hopes and prayers for what it might do, then and in ages to come, for the youth of the land. Still at the St. Francis Hotel, she mailed the talk, together with a short note, to George Crothers on the day she sailed.

San Francisco, February 15, 1905

Kind friend:

Enclosed you will please find my address which I would like the young student to read on the occasion of laying the cornerstone of the library. I have selected him. I thought it might please him to be so selected— it surely will give me pleasure to have him accept.

I have suggested to my brother to delay this event until the grounds around the building are in a better condition—say, until the last of March or in the month of April.

Your well wisher and friend,
Jane L. Stanford

Jane Stanford's address for the dedication of the new library was destined to be read posthumously on May 15, 1905, by Alexander Sherriffs, Class of '06. The text follows:

My health being somewhat impaired, I am advised by my physician to take a sea voyage to Honolulu. I regret this absence as it was my desire to be with you when laying the cornerstone of the University library. I deem this a fitting opportunity to express to you students a few of my views concerning the condition of affairs relating to the University generally.

No one can realize more fully than I the fact that the new library building, when completed, will be far beyond our present needs. Very many times I have pictured to myself the large number of spacious rooms

—the immense stack room, which will accommodate 1,000,000 volumes; its large central reading room, which will seat over 300 students at one time—and while this picture has pleased me, I also saw the opposite side, the need of very many books for the different departments of study. I fully and seriously realize how very sparse our present number of books will appear in the immensity of space. We need books at present more than anything else. My fondest wish has been to live long enough to give to you young students all the requisite buildings planned by the founders, and the erection of this library building marks the end of the material side in which I have been, for the past eight years, so intensely interested. But my love for the work so sacredly entrusted to me and my deep interest in the success of the students urged me to persevere, notwithstanding the other needs of the University at large.

The "stone age," which has been so frequently alluded to, no doubt was irritating and tedious to some connected with the University, but to me the erection of these stone buildings had a deep and important significance.

These noble buildings are not alone for the present but for ages to come, when generation after generation has passed and gone, and when, I hope and pray, these buildings will still stand and serve the purpose for which they have been erected, namely, for the benefit of the young of our land who will still be coming here to gain an education, and with time the required books will also come. We are young yet, only fourteen years old, a mere infant compared to grand old Harvard and Yale. I want each department to be supplied with its much needed books. I deeply and fully appreciate what a well selected and sufficient library means to a university. I also know that with a grand library we would be able to call to our assistance the ablest and best professors in the land, and our own honored professors could do better work and would be happier with the superior advantages. And the advantages offered by a grand library would draw to our far off shore here on the Pacific eager students, hungry for knowledge, from the East and West, just as the Harvard law library attracts to it enormous numbers who are fitting themselves for the profession of law—it has the best and largest in America. Johns Hopkins University has the best and largest medical library. I feel our deficiency more than I express.

I have not been so engrossed in the "stone age," the material side, as to ever lose sight of the spiritual. Not at all. I have never lost sight of all the internal needs, and I fully realize there is much to be done to bring the work here up to the expectations of the founders.

I would like to see our various departments more equally strengthened than they now are, and I hope to see departments of philosophy and ethics established, and other changes made in the interest of the humanities. Science must not overbalance the humanities as at present. I would like to see the spiritual side advanced, to be equaled up to the physical development. We must not lose sight of the fact that we are only beginners and are learning from our experiences what is wisest and best for our students. In the development and success of the student my soul's interests are centered; all else is only a means to that end. If there is one thing more I could do that would better them, make them stand out unique as noble men and women, helping their fellow men and women to live exemplary lives, how willingly, how gladly I would add all within my power to bring it about.

I think there is an interest that could well be added, and I have deplored its neglect in our work here—that is the development and cultivation of the soul life, the spiritual side of the nature of the students, which is by far one of the most important factors to be roused and educated. Without this we are not much above the level of the animal. It does not mean swaying or bending the young mind towards theology, creedism, or religious sectarianism of any kind. It means only to develop the soul seed lying dormant, waiting to be watered, nurtured, cared for, roused into life, and when that is accomplished it is a monitor to tell us what is right and what is wrong, for our conscience, when once awakened, never makes a mistake in admonishing us how to act.

While addressing you at this time, I deem it wise to embrace the opportunity of alluding to the work of the Memorial Church. I have the pleasure still before me of making a selection of a God-loving minister for the pulpit. I do not think the minister will wish an assistant—I hope he will not—but rather that he would consider it a wise plan to select students to assist him, a month at a time without compensation, students selected from the seniors who are willing to serve from love of duty, two or three at a time, if need be. What better way to draw church and school together? I would like to see the time come when no student would be willing to graduate unless he had served generously on the Church committee, and the helpers should not be chosen from the Christian Association exclusively.

University education levels up a student's standard of high honor toward humanity, gives him a better disciplined mind, makes him more philosophical, which is good and very apparent. But more is needed. Evil is defined as undeveloped good. Then let us strive one and all here

167

in this University to help awaken this God-planted soul germ, to develop evil into good. Here we are free to act according to our convictions and experiences. We are not trammeled by old traditions. Let us be guided always by the purest and best motives that actuate us for the benefit of the young students who place themselves under our care for development.

I am pleased with the normal healthy growth of the University, and I must again reiterate that a very large number of students is not my ambition. I am anxious to give the best possible in the way of professors, teachers, books, all that is requisite for each department in the way of instruments, tools, necessities of all kinds. But there should be a spirit of contentment, watchfulness, carefulness, self-discipline to help your neighbor if disabled in any way, and there should be respect for all that is given for your good. Above all else, no wastefulness. Then there will be pleasure in paying attention to your needs and our work will grow and God will smile upon us.

Before I close I wish to tell you I have already made provision for the future growth of the library, by the following arrangement made with the Board of Trustees.

On May 31st, 1899, I granted, assigned, transferred, and conveyed to the Trustees of the Leland Stanford Junior University, subject to certain terms and conditions set forth in the instrument conveying the same, all my jewels, consisting of diamonds, rubies, emeralds, and other precious stones, and directed that proceeds of the sale of said jewels, or so much thereof as might be necessary, be used in payment for the erection and completion of the Memorial Church, then about to be started.

Excepting such as were sold or otherwise disposed of prior to the first day of June 1903, said jewels were manually delivered to the Board. I was subsequently enabled to erect the Memorial Church without the necessity of resorting to the sale of these jewels.

In view of these facts and of my interest in the future development of the University Library, I have now requested the Trustees to establish and maintain a library fund, and upon the sale of said jewels, after my departure from this life, I desire that the proceeds therefrom be paid into said fund, and be preserved intact and invested in bonds or real estate as a part of the capital of the endowment, and that the income therefrom be used exclusively for the purchase of books and other publications.

I desire that this fund be known and designated as the Jewel Fund.

There has been created a Library Committee of the Board of Trustees, under the supervision of which all such purchase should be made.

It is to give you pleasure that I tell you the story of the Jewel Fund.

God bless you all is ever my prayer, for I well know prayer is the key that unlocks the doors of Heaven to us all.

Jane L. Stanford

San Francisco, California
February 14, 1905

In a second letter written to George Crothers on the day of her departure, Jane told him of her gratitude for all that he had done for her and for Stanford University.

San Francisco, February 15, 1905

Highly prized friend:

It would be doing my heart injustice were I to go away from my home, my sacred interests, the University without giving expression to all I feel in regard to your helpfulness to me for the past few years.

Your enthusiasm, your strict adherence to laws of the Grant, your cheer when I felt discouraged—for very many times I have experienced the feeling that my dear husband and I had over calculated our abilities to do all we fondly hoped for, because our means were insufficient; the calls for funds, the disappointment of others when I could not meet the demands, which seemed large to a novice, made me many times so discouraged I would ask myself the question, Have you undertaken something which in the end will be a failure? Have I assumed this duty of my own will? Are God and my loved ones in sympathy, sustaining me, or is it pride, self glorification that are actuating me? Or what can it be that keeps me here—no taste for the old allurements of life, no longing to stay from that country where my loved ones are dwelling?

Very many times, when battling with just such doubts, fears, questions, you would drop in to see me. Your topic of conversation always the University, you would tell me of its great future, its wonderful promise, its munificent endowment, what had already been done, what it had done for you and others you knew. I listened with surprise to hear your views. I thought at first they were the rosy views of youth, health, and happy life. I did not unburden myself; I did not want to disillusion you; I was glad that one young man had been benefited. I placed my son in your place and was thankful I knew you. I found you had let in a gleam of sunshine to me—things were not what they seemed. You had been a graduate, found good things that would stay with you through life—in fact, you opened the interior door of the University. Unfortunately, I heard only of wants.

All this I wanted to tell you before I go away. How much one can do for another and not know it—it is well to tell one of one's uplifting influence on others.

You know I am going away under peculiar circumstances, and I am not quite so sure of health and life as heretofore. Death in a natural way would not be a calamity for I have much and dearly loved ones waiting for my advent there, but I am startled and even horrified that any human beings feel that they have been injured to such an extent as to desire to revenge themselves in a way so heroic as has happened.

I have taken this opportunity to let you know how serviceable you have been to me, and I realize deeply how serviceable you are now and will be in the future to the University. You have it at heart, it is a part of your life. You know its needs; only its needs do we wish to supply—not unnecessary wants. We know we must be modest, not vainglorious—this you understand. I know God loves the meek and lowly of heart. We need be nothing else, and then He will guide, help, and strengthen us. And if we can each year succeed in sending forth from our University but one with your staid, well-poised, religious mind, I shall be satisfied. The Catholics say, and I believe it, "If we can save one soul we will be entitled to dwell ourselves in Heaven." I apply this same saying to every good act in life—it brings its reward.

I have said only a little of what I might truthfully add, but enough to set me at rest as to my duty towards you.

You were helpful in dark days, are helping still, and I hope our good, loving, Heavenly Father will spare you from sickness, sorrow, and death for very many years to come, and that you will always take the same deep interest in the University you now feel. Even though I "fall asleep" I shall awake in the fair land beyond, and I shall take with me fond remembrances and will pray for the privilege of doing something for the University and the students who love it.

With friendly greetings,

Your friend and well-wisher,
Jane L. Stanford

Lastly, a few hours before sailing, Jane wrote to May Hopkins:

San Francisco, February 15, 1905

My dear May:

Only a few words, my very dear friend, to let you know I have treasured all the sweet sympathy, all the priceless love, you have given me. I have wanted to see you since my illness, but I could not bring my mind to let you come. I have had more than sickness, a troubled heart—

I cannot tell you what you will know when a few more weeks have passed.

I felt more sorry than you can think that I had to recall the "at home" for dear Jennie, but it had to be. The doctor would not allow it.

Today I obey the doctor again and sail on the *Korea* for Honolulu and Japan. I need the sea voyage and the quiet. I go very unwillingly this time, for I wanted to be at Palo Alto through the beautiful spring and in June go to Europe and take Jennie.

I want your kind thoughts and Tim's and I need them. You and Tim have helped me so very much, loving me when old, heartbroken, lonely in my homes. I can't go away and not tell you all this that is in my heart. In a few hours I will be off.

Good-bye and God bless you, Tim, and dear Lydia.

Faithfully yours,

Jane L. Stanford

P.S. I have been in this hotel over a week, needing the quiet I could not get at home.

J.L.S.

The voyage to Honolulu was exceptionally rough but Jane Stanford, though depressed, was a seasoned traveler and withstood it well. She stayed at the Moana Hotel. Her spirits revived as each day she visited points of interest and each evening sat with Bertha Berner, her companion and secretary of many years, in a little arbor on a nearby pier to watch the glorious sunsets and afterward the rise of the full moon.

News from home was eagerly awaited and to help pass the time on the day before the arrival of the weekly mail from San Francisco, an excursion was planned. The hours passed pleasantly on a drive to the Pali and a picnic in a shaded grove close to the blue Pacific. More cheerful than she had been for some time, she spoke of the beauty of the scene and sang snatches of her favorite songs on the ride home. Having eaten heartily of a sumptuous lunch, topped off with several chocolate creams, she ate lightly that evening and retired early.

Just as much of Jane Stanford's life had been hard, notwithstanding all her advantages and achievements, so was her death. Some time in the quiet of the night she was heard to cry out in agony. Bertha Berner and May Hunt, her maid, hurried to her from their adjoining room and found her standing, clutching the door, and heard her exclaim in great distress, "I've been poisoned!"

While Miss Berner ran for the resident physician, May Hunt helped

Mrs. Stanford into a chair and began to rub her arms and legs. Bertha Berner returned, followed a few moments later by the doctor. Again saying she had been poisoned, Jane Stanford pitifully exclaimed, "This is a horrible death to die!" Pleadingly she asked Miss Berner to tell the doctor what had happened in San Francisco. Meanwhile, another physician who had been sent for joined the group. An emetic was given with good effect, followed by a hypodermic injection, after which Mrs. Stanford relaxed a little and seemed to be more comfortable. But soon her pain and accompanying spasm returned and a few moments later, Jane Stanford stopped breathing. In the excitement and confusion none of the participants took note of the time or duration of this distressing scene, but all agreed that the end came shortly before midnight on February 28, 1905. Mrs. Stanford was seventy-six years old.

David Starr Jordan's words on hearing of the death of Jane L. Stanford: "No one outside the University can understand the difficulties in her way in the final establishment of the University, and her patient deeds of self sacrifice can be known only to those who saw them from day to day. Some day the world may understand a part of this. It will then know her for the wisest, as well as the most generous, friend of learning in our time. What she did was always the best she could do. Wise, devoted and steadfast, prudent, patient, and just—every good word we can use was hers by right."

Just as it did in Jane Stanford's time, the lovely mosaic on the façade of Stanford Memorial Church depicting the Savior and his disciples still looks down on the red-tiled roofs and Inner Quadrangle of Stanford University. Outside this sanctum things have changed somewhat. New buildings to meet the requirements of the modern world seem to spring up continually over the wide campus. The paddocks and vineyards of the Palo Alto Farm are gone but the Arboretum still spreads its peaceful beauty over a goodly portion of the land.

Stanford University stands today in the forefront of those institutions representative of modern educational aims and practices, and the timeless ideals of its founders still permeate its lecture halls and laboratories. Much of the present campus scene would be new to Jane, but she would have no difficulty in recognizing the picture as a whole, and above all she could take pride in the countless number of her "boys and girls" who have led, and are leading, useful and creative lives because of her dedication and vision.

Epilogue

———◆◇◆———

JANE STANFORD'S BELIEF that she had been poisoned helped keep alive the controversy over the true cause of her death. Before going to bed on the fateful evening, she had asked Miss Berner to prepare a dose of bicarbonate of soda, a remedy she had taken periodically for many years for acid indigestion. Miss Berner dipped half a teaspoonful of soda from the bottle Mrs. Stanford had brought with her and placed it on her bedside table along with a tonic pill prescribed by Dr. Stanley Stillman which she had also been taking for years. The latter contained medicinal amounts of *nux vomica*, a mild heart and nerve stimulant containing minute amounts of strychnine and commonly prescribed for various chronic ailments of the aged.

An autopsy failed to reveal a cause of death. Minute amounts of strychnine were found in samples from the bottle of soda Mrs. Stanford had used and also in her stomach contents. These reports, together with her repeated outcry that she had been poisoned and the corroborative evidence of the attending physicians that her terminal symptoms had resembled those of strychnine poisoning, dominated the questions and answers at the inquest.

The verdict of the coroner's jury was inevitable; namely, that "Jane Lathrop Stanford came to her death . . . from strychnine poisoning, said strychnine having been introduced into a bottle of bicarbonate of soda with felonious intent by some person or persons to this jury unknown and of the contents of which bottle Jane Lathrop Stanford had partaken."

Immediately on hearing of Jane Stanford's death, Dr. Jordan and Timothy Hopkins sailed for Honolulu. Accompanying them were two highly reputable detectives, one a member of the San Francisco police force. After a comprehensive investigation of all the circumstances and exhaustive interviews with all the persons in any way involved in the events, they returned to San Francisco, bringing with them Mrs. Stan-

173

ford's vital organs and body fluids. These were submitted for study to a group of leading specialists headed by Dr. William Ophüls of Cooper Medical College. Their conclusion was that "the most probable cause of the death of Mrs. Stanford was chronic myocarditis (chronic disease of the heart muscles resulting from partial obstruction of the blood vessels of the heart)." This confirmed the view, which Dr. Jordan and his companions had reached independently, that Mrs. Stanford had not been poisoned.

Years later, while composing his memoirs, Dr. Jordan again reviewed the whole subject in a letter to Ray Lyman Wilbur, then the president of Stanford University.

"In my autobiography I shall not go into many details as to Mrs. Stanford's death. But I think that the University should have a record of the circumstances which led to the widespread idea that she was poisoned, and the simple explanations which the facts permit."

Dr. Jordan recounted the circumstances surrounding her death as already given, adding that the attending physician, "(an English remittance man, if not of good reputation), seemed dazed, as if under the influence of some drug. When told by Mrs. Stanford that she had been poisoned by strychnine, he tasted the bottle of soda and said something to the effect that it contained enough strychnine to kill a dozen men."

In view of the coroner's report that death had been due to strychnine poisoning, Jordan, Hopkins, and the two detectives had exhaustively pursued every lead in an attempt to reach the truth. Bertha Berner was held incommunicado in the Moana Hotel by the police authorities of Honolulu. The detectives gave her a rigid examination and declared her absolutely innocent of any evil. Hopkins and Jordan cross-questioned her independently and reached the same conclusion.

Among other things, they learned that the government analyst who had reported small amounts of strychnine in the soda Mrs. Stanford had taken and a trace of strychnine in her stomach was shortly afterward dismissed for fraudulent analysis. A competent physician who, however, had not seen Mrs. Stanford, after reviewing her symptoms reported that they did not tally in any degree with the rigors of muscle produced by strychnine. His diagnosis was a form of *angina pectoris*, due most probably to a rupture of the coronary artery. According to Dr. Jordan, this was later confirmed by the doctors at Cooper Medical College.

Jordan next reviewed the events that had taken place previously in San Francisco. Mr. Callundan, one of the detectives who had accompanied him to Honolulu, had found that a maid, temporarily employed by Mrs. Stanford, was subject to periodic attacks of mania and "that the chief subjects of her conversation with her associates turned on her experiences in the houses of the English aristocracy, with numerous anecdotes of those members of high society who had died from poisoning."

Dr. Jordan closed his letter with this comment: "I reached the conclusion that no one else could be under suspicion for the affair in San Francisco. Meeting Callundan at Placerville some time later, he told me that he believed that this phase of the mystery was fully solved. The poison was put into the Poland water in an insane freak. Meanwhile, as nothing could be absolutely proved, nothing was done in her case nor in the blunders or worse which took place at Honolulu. I have always regretted on Miss Berner's account that the Board did not see fit to publish the report of the surgeons of the Cooper Medical College, but there would be no gain in reopening those questions now after sixteen years."

Today there appears to be no good reason for not reporting the known facts.

Sources

JANE L. STANFORD's letters and papers are stored in containers in the Stanford University Archives. The first two boxes hold six large volumes of personal letters, papers, addresses, and telegrams, mostly her own communications but also a number from correspondents, including David Starr Jordan, Susan B. Anthony, individual Stanford students, C.P. Huntington, Joseph H. Choate, Andrew D. White, and others. The material is arranged chronologically and each volume has a complete index giving the date, addresser and addressee, and main content of each missive.

The letters reproduced in the text, with a few exceptions, also appear chronologically. The exceptions were made when it seemed important to keep together subject matter rather than time periods. Nevertheless, by noting the date, addresser and recipient, and contents of a given letter in the text, a glance through the index of the appropriate volume in the Archives will quickly disclose the original.

The original of Jane Stanford's letter to the student R.R. Culver is in the California Historical Society's Archives. Her last letter to George E. Crothers is reproduced from a copy in the flyleaf of Crothers' account of the founding of the University, his gift to the Pacific-Union Club library.

A third container has loose letters and material not otherwise pinpointed. The five letters reproduced in Chapters III and IV, including Jane Stanford's earliest available one to Leland written in 1869 and the one from Florence, Italy, to the Timothy Hopkinses shortly before Leland Jr. died in 1884, are in a folder in this box. H.C. Nash's essay on Jane's early years and her charitable contributions are also in Container III.

Copies of the Stanford student paper, the Daily Palo Alto, of April 22, 1903, describing Jane Stanford's meeting with and talk to the women students, and the issue of January 25, 1903, which gives a full account of the dedication of Memorial Church, including the sermons of the Rev. Heber Newton and Dr. D. Charles Gardner, are in the newspaper files in the University's Main Library.

Jane Stanford's newspaper interview is from the *San Francisco Examiner*, October 18, 1901. Senator Stanford's Herald Bureau interview is from Elliott's *Stanford University*, pp. 583–84.

A complete copy of the Coroner's inquest on the death of Jane Lathrop Stanford held in Honolulu on the 6th, 7th, and 9th days of March 1905 is in the Stanford University Archives. The folder containing this document also has a copy of the letter from Dr. Jordan to Ray Lyman Wilbur, excerpts from which are quoted in the Epilogue.

Statements of fact relating to the University and those most closely involved in its story came from many sources. The most useful and carefully documented accounts are those of Orrin Leslie Elliott and George T. Clark. Elliott, who was Stanford's first registrar, had the good fortune to know the principals and witness the events of which he wrote. Clark, the director of University Libraries, came to Stanford in 1907 when memories of the founders' activities were still fresh. Others who gave permanence to the spoken record are David Starr Jordan, Edith Mirrielees, George E. Crothers, Ray Lyman Wilbur, and many more. They are listed in the bibliography.

Bibliography

Albany Female Academy. *Circular and Catalogue of the Albany Female Academy*, 1845. In the Stanford University Archives.

Berner, Bertha. *Mrs. Leland Stanford, an Intimate Account*. Stanford, Calif.: Stanford University Press, 1935.

Branner, J.C. "One of Mrs. Stanford's Ideals." Founders' Day Address, March 10, 1917.

Clark, George T. *Leland Stanford*. Stanford, Calif.: Stanford University Press, 1931.

Crothers, George E. "Founding of the Leland Stanford Junior University." Reprinted from the April 1932 issue of *Americana*. San Francisco: A.M. Robertson, 1932.

———. "The Educational Ideals of Jane Lathrop Stanford, Co-founder of the Leland Stanford Junior University." An address delivered before the 1933 California Conference of the Daughters of the American Revolution.

Elliott, Orrin Leslie. *Stanford University, The First Twenty-Five Years*. Stanford, Calif.: Stanford University Press, 1937.

Evans, Cerinda W. *Collis Potter Huntington*. 2 vols. Newport News, Va.: The Mariners' Museum, 1954.

Field, Charles K., and Irwin, Will H. *Stanford Stories*. New York: Doubleday, Page & Co., 1903.

Fish, J.C.L. "Typhoid Fever Epidemic at Palo Alto, California." A report made to the Palo Alto Board of Health by the president of the board, 1905.

Flexner, Eleanor. *Century of Struggle, The Woman's Rights Movement in the United States*. Cambridge, Mass.: The Belknap Press of Harvard University Press, 1959.

Harper, Ida Husted, ed. *The History of Woman Suffrage*. Vol. 6, 1900–1920. New York: National American Woman Suffrage Association; printed and bound by J.J. Little & Ives Co.

Hole, Judith & Levine, Ellen. *Rebirth of Feminism*. New York: Quadrangle Books, 1971. A *New York Times* publication.

Jordan, David Starr. "The Call of the Twentieth Century: An Address to Young Men." American Unitarian Association, Boston, 1903.

———. "The Story of a Good Woman, Jane Lathrop Stanford." American Unitarian Association, Boston, 1912.

———. *The Days of a Man*. 2 vols. Yonkers-on-Hudson, N.Y.: World Book Co., 1922.

Kraus, George. *High Road to Promontory, Building the Central Pacific*. Palo Alto, Calif.: American West Publishing Co., 1969.

Lavender, David. *The Great Persuader*. Garden City, N.Y.: Doubleday & Co., 1970.

Lyons, Louise S., ed. *Who's Who Among the Women of California*. San Francisco: Security Publishing Co., 1922.

Mirrielees, Edith R., ed. *Stanford Mosaic*. Stanford, Calif.: Stanford University Press, 1962.

———. *Stanford, The Story of a University*. New York: G.P. Putnam's Sons, 1959.

Mosher, Clelia Duel. "Notes Concerning Jane E. Lathrop (Mrs. Leland Stanford) who attended the Albany Female Academy in the 1840s." 1939. In the Stanford University Archives.

Noun, Louise R. *Strong-Minded Women, the Emergence of the Woman-Suffrage Movement in Iowa*. Ames, Iowa: Iowa State University Press, 1969.

Siegel, Alberta E., in collaboration with Carr, Ronald G. "Education of Women at Stanford University." From *The Study of Education at Stanford, Vol. 7*, 1969.

Sinclair, Andrew. *The Better Half, The Emancipation of the American Woman*. New York: Harper and Row, 1965.

Stanford University. *Stanford Memorial Church*. Second printing, with revisions, 1968.

———. *Stanford University Trustees Manual*. Seventh Edition, 1964.

Stanton, Elizabeth Cady; Anthony, Susan B.; and Gage, Matilda Joslyn. *History of Woman Suffrage. Vol. 1*. Rochester, N.Y.: Susan B. Anthony, 1887.

Starr, Kevin. *Americans and the California Dream, 1850–1915*. New York, Oxford University Press, 1973.

Stillman, J.D.B. *Seeking the Golden Fleece*. San Francisco and New York: A. Roman and Co., 1877.

———. *The Horse in Motion as Shown by Instantaneous Photography*. Executed and published under the auspices of Leland Stanford. Boston: James R. Osgood & Co., 1882.

Tutorow, Norman E. *Leland Stanford, Man of Many Careers*. Menlo Park, Calif.: Pacific Coast Publishers, 1971.

179